Madame Monsigny

Mythology

A History of the Fabulous Deities of the Ancients - designed to facilitate the study of

history, poetry, painting, etc

Madame Monsigny

Mythology
A History of the Fabulous Deities of the Ancients - designed to facilitate the study of history, poetry, painting, etc

ISBN/EAN: 9783337178703

Printed in Europe, USA, Canada, Australia, Japan

Cover: Foto ©Andreas Hilbeck / pixelio.de

More available books at **www.hansebooks.com**

MYTHOLOGY;

OR,

A HISTORY

OF

THE FABULOUS DEITIES

OF

THE ANCIENTS:

DESIGNED TO FACILITATE THE STUDY

OF

HISTORY,

POETRY, PAINTING, &c.

London:

PRINTED FOR WILLIAM RICHARDSON, ROYAL-
EXCHANGE.

To MRS. PACKE.

MADAM,

THE approbation with which you have been pleafed to honour this little WORK, and the hope that it may be of fome utility to thofe young perfons of our fex, who are as yet unacquainted with the STUDY of MYTHOLOGY, have been my principal inducements for making it public. You are well acquainted with the motives that engaged me to attempt a compilation of this nature. Convinced that a knowledge of what have been the fuperftitions and fables of the Ancients is abfolutely neceffary, in order to comprehend moft of the fubjects of POETRY, PAINTING, &c. I felt *that* education muft be imperfect from which this ftudy is excluded; yet I was embarraffed what books to make choice

choice of for the inftruction of my pupils. I knew of none which I could
with propriety put into their hands, fince
I had not met with any on the fubject,
at leaft any fuch as could give them all
the information I wifhed, and which were
not liable to the fame objection, I mean
the indecencies they abound with. Thefe
confiderations, as you know, Madam,
prompted me to attempt this work, though
at firft with a fole view of being myfelf
the better enabled to fulfil the duties of
the truft which you had confided to me,
and of neglecting nothing which appeared to me worthy the attention of
one who undertakes the important charge
of EDUCATION. In this compilation
it has been my care to obviate the above
objection, by rejecting, as much as it depended on me to do, what I have found
exceptionable in books of this kind, and
at the fame time to give a clear and dif-
tinct account of all the principal PER-
SONAGES and EVENTS of the FABU-
LOUS HISTORY. You, as well as others
of

of my friends, have judged it might become more generally useful than I had at firſt imagined, or intended ; I therefore offer it to the Public, and if it ſhould meet with any ſucceſs, it is to the encouragement and aſſiſtance you have given me, that I am indebted for it. I cannot help feeling, on this occaſion, the timidity natural to a perſon unaccuſtomed to ſtand forth in ſo conſpicuous a light, and perhaps too unequal to the undertaking ; but however unſucceſsful this attempt may prove, I ſhall eſteem myſelf gratified by the generous protection granted it by you, and by being permitted to make this public profeſſion of the perfect Reſpect, Gratitude, and Attachment with which I am,

MADAM,

Your much obliged and

Moſt obedient Servant,

MARY MONSIGNY.

INTRODUCTION.

AS an introduction to this work, it may not be improper to give my young readers fome account of the origin and progrefs of idolatry.

We learn from facred hiftory, that mankind degenerated very early from the worfhip of the God: they were, for their crimes, deprived of that knowledge of him which had at firft been implanted in their minds by himfelf. Thus abandoned to the guidance of their own weak reafon and vain imaginations, they funk by degrees into univerfal depravity, and their enormities became fo great, as to provoke their Almighty Creator to deftroy the world which he had formed.

After the deluge, and when men began again to multiply, and to form focieties, it is believed

they

they were not without some kind of religious
worship; but being chiefly occupied by those
cares which were necessary to the preservation
of their existence, they were incapable of dis-
tinguishing, in the connexion and harmony of
the different parts of the universe, the power,
wisdom, and goodness of its great Author.
They had no idea of one *only* God, the Creator
of all things, present in all places, and existing
eternally by his own power. Ignorance gave
birth to superstition, and superstition produced
fear and idolatry. Unable to penetrate into
the causes of events which they saw and experienced, and more sensibly affected by the evils
which they suffered, than by the good which they
enjoyed; they began to conceive there must be
some secret power above them, some Divinity,
whose protection and favour it was necessary to
implore. Sacrifices were offered to this unknown
object of their adoration, which they worshiped
with more dread than affection, and which they
began to represent under various forms, according to the different ideas they entertained of
him, and frequently it was under those of the
most noxious, and even of the vilest of animals.
In some parts of Greece, as well as in Egypt, it
was the figure of a serpent, and sometimes the
serpent itself, which they made choice of for
                                        their

their protector. They believed it possessed of superior intelligence, because, seeing that it sometimes changed its skin, they imagined it had the power of maintaining itself in perpetual youth, and was therefore immortal. Many other animals, insects, and even inanimate things, were regarded with religious veneration, particularly among the Egyptians. Their principal divinity was the God Apis, which was no other than an ox, and which they worshiped with great solemnity. He had a superb temple in the city of Memphis, and a great number of priests who offered incense on his altar.

Those who inhabited the sea-coasts, observing the tides overflow their shores at the full moon, believed the moon to be the cause of what happened at the times of its different phases, and looked up to it as a powerful Deity. The Asiatics adored the stars, and the Chaldeans, before the first Zoroaster, rendered homage to the Sun, as the Peruvians have since done in another hemisphere. This error must have been very natural to man, since it has had so many sectators both in Asia and America. That glorious luminary which animates all nature, seemed to claim his gratitude for the benefits it dispensed, and of which they imagined it to be

the

the fole author. In effect, it is not extraordinary, that different nations fhould have imbibed the fame prejudices, with refpect to fuch things as affect the fenfes, and ftrike the imagination. Thus the noife, the effects of thunder, were attributed to the power of a fuperior Being, inhabitant of the air.

It is not fo natural to make a *God* of a *Man*, whom we have feen born like ourfelves, fuffer like ourfelves, all the miferies to which human nature is liable, in fine, die, and become food for worms; yet this happened with almoft all nations, after the revolution of many ages. Ninus, king of the Affyrians, is faid to have eftablifhed this kind of worfhip, in honour of his father Belus, or Nimrod, grandfon of Noah, and founder of the city of Babylon. To render his name immortal, Ninus caufed a ftatue of him to be made, and commanded his fubjects to pay the fame reverence to it, as they would have done to Belus, if ftill alive; ordaining likewife, that this ftatue fhould be a fanctuary for offenders, and that it fhould not be lawful to force them from it to punifhment. So great was the veneration which this privilege procured to the memory of the dead prince, that he was believed immortal, and therefore worfhiped

fhiped as a God under the name of Bel. A magnificent temple was built for him at Babylon, and dedicated with many facrifices in the two thoufandth year of the world. This, according to many writers, was the commencement of idolatry; and the Bel of the Affyrians, was afterwards the Jupiter of the Greeks and Romans. From this peftilential fource, the contagion diffufed itfelf into almoft all parts of the world, and every nation had its Gods. A man who had performed great actions, who had rendered important fervices to his country, was deified after his death, and there was fcarcely a young warrior of diftinguifhed valour, who was not reputed the fon of a God. Thus Bacchus, Perfeus, Hercules, &c. were accounted fons of Jupiter, and Alexander the Great was more vain of this title, which he obtained from the Oracle of Jupiter-Ammon, than of all his conquefts. Princes, actuated by a falfe ambition, and an inordinate love of fame, in order to perpetuate their names to future ages, and to obtain divine honours, caufed ftatues of themfelves to be made; and fuch was the fervile flattery of fubjects, that they fcrupled not to erect altars to them, on which they offered incenfe as to their Gods, and this frequently while they were yet living.

The

The female Deities were not lefs numerous than thofe of the other fex. Semiramis was worfhiped by the Affyrians, and Ifis by the Egyptians. Many of the Goddeffes were efteemed equal in power to any of the Gods except Jupiter alone, who was regarded as fupreme over Gods and Men.

When Arts and fciences began to prevail, and a tafte for elegant and beautiful compofitions had difplayed itfelf among mankind, the Poets (particularly Homer) embellifhed thefe fictions, and encreafed their credit, by their lively defcriptions and harmonious numbers. They affigned to each Deity his particular attributes and functions; they recorded the actions of Gods and Heroes, and celebrated their praifes, yet fo far were many of thofe actions from meriting praife, that they would have difgraced men. Not only human weakneffes, but the moft fhocking vices, were attributed to thefe fuppofed Divinities; and the immortal Gods, whofe province they believed it to reward virtue, and to punifh crimes, inftead of being themfelves held up as *patterns* of purity and perfection, were reprefented as fubject to human paffions, and capable of committing the moft indecent actions. Such examples were

not

not calculated to correct the degenerate nature of man, or to animate him with refolution and firmnefs to combat againft the feductions of pleafure, or the tyranny of the paffions. If we reflect upon the miferable gloom of ignorance and fuperftition with which the world was overfpread in thofe early ages, we fhall no longer wonder at the enormities that were committed in it, and we fhall be more inclined to commiferate the blindnefs of thofe idolaters, than to condemn them for what was the natural effect of that blindnefs. But what is truly worthy our admiration, is the many bright examples of moral rectitude and of heroic virtue which even thofe times produced. Hiftory has tranfmitted to us the names and deeds of men of every rank and denomination in the pagan world, which Chriftians need not blufh to imitate. There we read of kings who were the protectors and fathers of their people; of citizens, who facrificed their own interefts, their refentments, nay, even their lives to the public good; of wife legiflators, who laboured fincerely and effectually to promote the happinefs of mankind, and of philofophers, whofe ftudies were all directed to the fame object. Some of thefe laft, endued with extraordinary powers of reafoning, and fuperior to prejudice, feem to have been almoft

capable

capable of breaking the fhackles of idolatry,
and of piercing the dark cloud which prevented
men from knowing and adoring their Creator.
To the comprehenfive mind of a Socrates and
a Plato, every object in nature announced a
Being infinitely wife and juft, fupreme in power,
tranfcendent in goodnefs, eternal, and unchange-
able. The firft of thefe, and the greateft of all
philofophers, was accufed of making innova-
tions in the religion of the Greeks, and of ri-
diculing the multitude of Gods which the Athenians worfhiped. For this crime he was condemned to drink hemlock. The compofure
with which he met death, has been much celebrated, though this was the refult, not of his
fuperior genius and extenfive knowledge, but
of his irreproachable life and exemplary virtue.
He converfed with his difciples (who attended
him in his prifon), and continued to inftruct
them to his laft moments. He reproved their
excefs of forrow on his account, and when one
of them was expreffing his grief at the hardnefs
of his fate, in that he was to fuffer, though innocent, the philofopher replied, " Would you
then have me die guilty?" Socrates died about
400 years before Chrift, in the 70th year of
his age.

Such

Such examples among Pagans are proper to animate the zeal of Chriſtians. If nature and reaſon, unaided by revelation, could operate thus happily, what ought not we to perform? The peruſal of the following pages may likewiſe ſuggeſt ſome uſeful reflections, and be attended with more ſolid advantage than it ſeems at firſt to promiſe. Even the Study of the Heathen Mythology may teach us to ſet a higher value upon our pure religion; for, while we conſider theſe abſurd fictions, and deplore the condition of thoſe who were educated in the belief of them, and born as it were ſlaves to folly and extravagance, muſt we not be filled with that gratitude which a ſenſe of the ineſtimable bleſſings we enjoy ſo naturally inſpires towards him, who is the fountain of light, and the author of all good; who has at length vouchſafed to diſſipate thoſe clouds of error, and brightly to illuminate the path which he has deſtined us to tread?

It muſt not be imagined that all the Deities, and other perſonages, whoſe names and actions are found in the fabulous hiſtory, are abſolutely fictitious. Many of them had a real exiſtence, though a very different one from that which is there aſcribed to them. They were either

Princes

Princes, Generals of Armies, or other perfons whofe lives and characters were diftinguifhed by extraordinary events or great exploits. The memory of fuch men was perpetuated, and their actions celebrated with enthufiafm and much exaggeration, till (as has been already obferved) they were at length regarded as more than hu-man, and venerated as divine.

The Deities worfhiped by the Romans were divided into three ranks or claffes. The firft clafs was that of the fuperior or felect Gods, which were honoured with the higheft degree of adoration, becaufe they were believed to be eminent in power and glory above the others, and to prefide more particularly over the affairs of this world: twelve of thefe were called *Confentees*, becaufe in affairs of great im-portance they were admitted by Jupiter into his council. Six of them were males, and fix females. Their names were as follows: Ju-piter, Apollo, Mercury, Mars, Neptune, and Vulcan ; Juno, Minerva, Diana, Venus, Vefta, and Ceres. Their ftatues were placed in the Forum at Rome, and they were com-monly called, without other diftinction, the twelve Gods: they were thought to prefide over the twelve months of the year, to each was al-
lotted

lotted a month, January to Juno, February to Neptune, March to Minerva, April to Venus, May to Apollo, June to Mercury, July to Jupiter, Auguſt to Ceres, September to Vulcan, October to Mars, November to Diana, and December to Veſta. They preſided likewiſe over the twelve celeſtial ſigns. To theſe muſt be added Bacchus, Saturn, Janus, and Pluto, who were alſo reckoned among the ſuperior divinities.

The ſecond claſs comprehend thoſe of inferior power and dignity, and ſuch of the human race whoſe virtues or heroic deeds had obtained them immortality, and a place among the Gods. Theſe were very numerous.

The third and lower claſs was innumerable. It conſiſted chiefly of thoſe who were ſtiled Sylvan Deities, who inhabited the woods, gardens, fountains, &c. The Nereides, or Sea-Nymphs, and the Penates, or Houſehold Gods, the Genii, the Virtues, &c.

In order to avoid confuſion, and to give the greater perſpicuity to this work. I ſhall divide the Deities, &c. into ſix diſtinct claſſes, as follows :

I. The

I. The Celeftial Gods and Goddeffes.

II. The Terreftrial Divinities.

III. The Sylvan and Domeftic Deities, &c.

IV. The Gods of theSea; or, the Marine

　　　Gods.

V. The Infernal Gods, &c. and

VI. The Demi Gods, Heroes, &c. &c.

MYTHOLOGY.

CELESTIAL GODS.

JUPITER	MARS
APOLLO	BACCHUS
MERCURY	CUPID.

JUPITER.

THE firſt of the celeſtial Deities was Jupiter, called the King and Father of both Gods and Men. He was the ſon of Saturn and Ops. According to the Mythologiſts, Jupiter was ſaved from deſtruction by his mother, and entruſted to the care of the Corybantes. Saturn, who had received the kingdom of the world from his brother Titan, on condition of not raiſing male children, devoured his ſons as ſoon as born; but Ops ſecreted Jupiter from her huſband's cruelty, and gave a ſtone to Saturn, which he devoured, ſuppoſing it to be the child. Jupiter was educated in a cave on Mount Ida, in Crete, and fed, ſome ſay, upon goats milk, according to others upon honey. That his cries might not reach the ears of Saturn, the Corybantes, by the command of Ops, beat drums and cymbals continually. When Jupiter was very young, he made war againſt the Titans, who had impriſoned his father, becauſe he had brought up male children. He was victo-

B   rious

rious, and procured Saturn his liberty; but Saturn becoming jealous of the growing power of his son, conspired against him, and was, for this treachery, driven from his kingdom, and fled for safety to Latium. After which, Jupiter divided the empire of the world with his two brothers, Neptune and Pluto, who had, like him, been preserved by Ops. He reserved for himself the sole dominion of heaven and earth, and gave the empire of the sea to Neptune, and that of the infernal regions to Pluto. The Giants, who were the sons of the earth, rebelled against Jupiter, in order to avenge the death of the Titans, whom he had slain. They hurled immense rocks, and heaped up mountains upon mountains, thinking to scale heaven. So that the Gods, to avoid their fury, fled to Egypt, and there assumed the forms of different animals. This tradition was the cause of the veneration which the Egyptians preserved for so many animals, and of the adoration which they paid them. Jupiter, however, by the assistance of Hercules, entirely overpowered the whole race of the Giants, and inflicted on them the several punishments of which we shall speak hereafter.

Jupiter had many wives of which the following are the names; Metis, one of the Oceanides; Themis,

Themis, a daughter of Cœlus and Terra, and the mother of Dice ; Irene, Eunomia, the Parcæ, &c. Erynome, one of the Oceanides, and mother of the Graces ; Mnemofyne, a daughter of Cœlus and Terra, the mother of the Nine Mufes. He likewife efpoufed his fifter Juno, and fhe feems to have been the only one of his wives who had any fhare in his power and dignity. Jupiter became fenfible likewife to the charms of many other beauties, as well mortals as divinities. The names of the principal of thefe were ; Latona, the daughter of Cœus the Titan, or, according to Homer, of Saturn. She was the mother of Apollo and Diana. Ceres, the Goddefs of Corn and of Harvefts. She was likewife the daughter of Saturn, and was the mother of Proferpine. Danae, the daughter of Acrifius, king of Argos, and the mother of Perfeus. Danae was confined by her father in a brazen tower, on account of an oracle which had foretold, that his daughter's fon would put him to death. Jupiter eluded the precaution, and introduced himfelf to Danae, by changing himfelf into a fhower of gold. Antiope, the daughter of Nyƈteus, king of Thebes, had twin fons by Jupiter ; thefe were Amphion and Zethus. The God took the form of a fwan, to introduce himfelf to Leda, the wife of

Tyndarus,

Tyndarus, king of Sparta. Leda brought forth two eggs ; from one of thefe fprung Pollux and Helena, and from the other Caftor and Clytemneftra.   The two former were deemed the offspring of Jupiter, and the others claimed Tyndarus as their father.   He carried off Europa, the daughter of Agenor, king of Phenicia, in the form of a bull, and bore her on his back over the fea to Crete.   She became the mother of Minos, Sarpedon, and Rhadamanthus.   He affumed the habit of Diana, to feduce one of her nymphs, Califto, daughter of Lycaon, king of Arcadia.   Juno, enraged with jealoufy, changed Califto into a bear ; but Jupiter made her a conftellation of Heaven with her fon Arcas, under the name of the Bear.   He changed himfelf into a flame of fire, to warm the heart of Ægina, the daughter of Afopus, who was a fon of Neptune, and by her had Æacus.   He took the fhape of Amphytrion, to gain the affections of his wife Alcmena, who was the mother of the Great Hercules.   Electra, one of the Oceanides, wife of Atlas, and mother of Dardanus, by Jupiter.   Maia, the daughter of Atlas, was the mother of the god Mercury ; fhe was one of the Pleiades, and the moft luminous of the feven fifters.   Niobe, a daughter of Phoroneus, king of Peloponnefus.   She had

had a fon called Argus, who gave his name
to Argia, or Argolis, a country of Peloponnefus. Laodamia, a daughter of Bellerophon. She
had a fon called Sarpedon, who was king of
Lycia : he went to the Trojan war, to affift
Priam againft the Greeks, where he was attended by his friend Glaucus: he was killed
by Patroclus, after having greatly diftinguifhed
by himfelf by his valour. According to fome
Mythologifts, the prince who affifted Priam,
was Sarpedon, the fon of Jupiter, by Europa.
Protogenia, a daughter of Deucalion and
Pyrrha, had likewife a fon by Jupiter, Æthlius,
who was the father of Endymion, Semele, a
daughter of Cadmus and of Hermione, the
daughter of Mars and Venus ; fhe was tenderly
beloved by Jupiter, but Juno, determined to
punifh this rival, and the rather, becaufe fhe
hated all the houfe of Cadmus. She took the
form of Boroe, Semele's nurfe, to vifit her.
Semele lifttened to her artful fuggeftions, by
which fhe was perfuaded to entreat her lover,
as a proof that he really was Jupiter, to vifit
her with the fame pomp and fplendour as when
he approached the queen of Heaven. This rafh
requeft was heard with horror by the God; but,
as he had already fworn by the Styx, to grant
whatever fhe required, he came to her attended

by

by the clouds, the lightning, and thunder-bolts. The mortal nature of Semele could not endure so much majesty, and she was instantly consumed with fire. The child, however, of which she was pregnant, was preserved by Mercury, and was called Bacchus. Some say that Jupiter enclosed him in his own thigh, till the time of his birth was accomplished. Io, the daughter of Inachus, who founded the kingdom of Argos, was priestess of Juno. Jupiter became enamoured of her, but Juno, jealous of his intrigues, discovered the object of his affection, and surprised him in the company of Io. Jupiter changed his mistress into a beautiful heifer; but the Goddess, who perceived the fraud, obtained from her husband the animal, whose beauty she pretended to admire, and Juno committed her to the care of Argus, who had an hundred eyes. Jupiter, in the mean time, anxious for the safety of Io, sent Mercury to destroy Argus, and to restore her to liberty. Io, though freed from the vigilance of her keeper, was still persecuted by Juno, who sent a malicious insect to torment her. She wandered over a great part of the earth, and crossed the sea, till at length she stopped on the banks of the Nile, still exposed to the torments of Juno's insect. Here, at her entreaties, Jupiter restored

reſtored her to her proper form, and ſhe brought forth Epaphus ; ſhe afterwards married Telegonus, king of Egypt, or, according to ſome, Oſiris, and ſhe treated her ſubjects with ſo much mildneſs and humanity, that, after her death, ſhe received divine honours, and was worſhipped under the name of Iſis.

The power of Jupiter was ſuppoſed to extend over all the Deities, and every thing was ſubſervient to his will, except the Fates. From him mankind received their bleſſings and their miſeries, and they believed him to be acquainted with every thing paſt, preſent, and to come. The ſins of mankind, it is related, were become ſo enormous, that Jupiter reſolved to viſit the earth, in order to puniſh wickedneſs and impiety. He came to Arcadia, where he was announced as a God, and the people began to pay proper adoration to his divinity. Lycaon, however, the king of that country, who uſed to ſacrifice all ſtrangers to his wanton cruelty, laughed at the pious prayers of his ſubjects, and to prove the divinity of the God, he ſerved up human fleſh on his table. This impiety ſo irritated Jupiter, that he inſtantly deſtroyed the houſe of Lycaon, and changed him into a wolf.

B 4   The

The worſhip of Jupiter was univerſal, and ſurpaſſed that of all the other Gods in ſolemnity. His altars were not ſtained with the blood of human victims, like thoſe of Saturn and Diana; but he was pleaſed with the ſacrifice of goats, ſheep, and white bulls. The Oak is ſacred to him, becauſe he firſt taught mankind to live upon acorns. He is generally repreſented as ſitting upon a golden or ivory throne, holding in one hand thunderbolts, juſt ready to be hurled; and, in the other, a ſceptre of cypreſs. His looks expreſs majeſty, his beard flows long and neglected, and the eagle ſtands with expanded wings at his feet. He is ſometimes repreſented with the upper parts of his body naked, and thoſe below carefully covered; as if to ſhew that he is viſible to the Gods above, but is concealed from the ſight of the inhabitants of the earth. At Olympia he was repreſented with a crown like olive-branches: his mantle was variegated with different flowers, particularly by the lilly, and the eagle perched on the top of the ſceptre which he held in his hand. The Cretans repreſented Jupiter without ears, to ſignify, that the ſovereign maſter of the univerſe ought not to give a partial hearing to any particular perſon, but be equally candid and propitious to all. At Lacedæmon, he appeared

with

with four heads, that he might feem to hear with greater readinefs the different prayers and folicitations which were daily addreffed to him from every part of the earth. Jupiter had feveral oracles, the moft celebrated of which were thofe of Dodona, and Ammon in Lybia. It is faid, that having ordered Vulcan to open his head, Minerva, the Goddefs of Wifdom and of Arms, fprung from his brain.

The furnames of Jupiter were numerous, many of which he received from the places or functions over which he prefided. He was feverally called Jupiter Ammon, Feretrias, Inventor, Elicius, Capitolinus, Latialis, Piftor, Sponfor, Herceus, Anxurus, Victor, Maximus, Optimus, Olympius, Fluvialis, &c. but moft commonly he is called Jove or Jupiter.

According to Varro, Diodorus, and Cicero, there were many perfons of the name of Jupiter ; and, it is conjectured, that to him of Crete, who paffed for the fon of Saturn and Ops, the actions of all the reft have been attributed.

APOLLO,

APOLLO.

APOLLO, fon of Jupiter and Latona, called alfo Phœbus or Sol, which is the fun. According to Cicero there were four perfons of this name. The firft was fon of Vulcan, and the tutelary God of the Athenians. The fecond was the fon of Corybas, and born in Crete, for the dominion of which he difputed even with Jupiter himfelf. The third was fon of Jupiter and Latona, and came from the nations of the Hyperboreans to Delphi. The fourth was born in Arcadia, and called Nomion, becaufe he gave laws to the inhabitants. To the fon of Jupiter and Latona, all the actions of the others feem to have been attributed. The Apollo, fon of Vulcan, was the fame as the Orus of the Egyptians, and was the moft ancient; from him the actions of the three others, who feem to have been of a Grecian origin, have been copied. The tradition, that the fon of Jupiter was born in the floating ifland of Delos, is taken from the Egyptian Mythology, which afferts, that the fon of Vulcan, which is fuppofed

to

to be Orus, was faved by his mother Ifis, from the perfecution of Typhon, and entrufted to the care of Latona, who concealed him in the ifland of Chemmis. When Latona was pregnant, Juno, ever jealous of her hufband's amours, raifed the ferpent Python to torment Latona, who was refufed a place where to give birth to her children, till Neptune was moved at the feverity of her fate, and raifed the ifland of Delos from the bottom of the fea, where fhe brought forth Apollo and Diana. The former, as foon as he was born, deftroyed with arrows the ferpent Python, who perfecuted his mother, hence he was called Pythius. He was accounted the God of all the fine Arts; of medicine, mufic, poetry, and eloquence; of all which he was deemed the inventor. He had received from Jupiter the knowledge of futurity, and he was the only one of the Gods, whofe oracles were in general repute all over the world.

When his fon, Efculapius, had been killed with the thunders of Jupiter, for raifing the dead to life, Apollo, in his refentment, killed the Cyclops who had fabricated the thunder-bolts. Jupiter was incenfed at this violence, and he banifhed Apollo from Heaven, and deprived

B 6   him

him of his dignity. The exiled Deity came to Admetus, king of Theſſaly, and hired himſelf to be one of his ſhepherds, in which ignoble employment he remained nine years, and from which circumſtance he was called the God of Shepherds. During his reſidence in Theſſaly, he rewarded the kind treatment of Admetus. He gave him a chariot drawn by a lion and a bull, with which he was able to obtain in marriage, Alceſte, the daughter of Pelias; and ſoon after, the Parcæ, at the requeſt of Apollo, granted that Admetus might be redeemed from death, if another perſon laid down his life for him. Apollo aſſiſted Neptune in building the walls of Troy; and when Laomedon, the king of the country, refuſed him the promiſed reward, he deſtroyed the inhabitants by a peſtilence : he, with his ſiſter Diana, killed in one day, the ſeven ſons and ſeven daughters of Niobe, as well as her huſband, becauſe ſhe had the imprudence, not only to prefer herſelf to Latona, whom ſhe deſpiſed on account of her having had only two children, but ſhe even inſulted her, and ridiculed the worſhip which was paid to her, alledging that ſhe had a better claim to altars and ſacrifices than the mother of Apollo and Diana. Niobe, ſtruck with mortal grief at the ſudden loſs of all ſhe held ſo

dear,

dear, wept inceffantly, and was at laft chang'd into a ftone. Marfyas, a celebrated piper of Celænæ, in Phrygia, was flead alive by Apollo, for having dared to challenge him to a trial of his fkill as a mufician.   Midas, a king of Phrygia, having had the imprudence to aflert, that the God Pan was fuperior to Apollo in finging and playing on the flute, the offended Deity, for this rafh opinion, changed his ears into thofe of an afs, to fhew his ignorance and ftupidity.   Midas endeavoured to conceal this difgrace from his fubjects, but it was perceived by one of his fervants, who being unable to keep the fecret, yet afraid to reveal it (apprehending the king's refentment), he dug a hole in the earth, and putting his mouth to it, whifpered thefe words, " *King Midas has affes ears,*" then filling up the place he left it ; but the poets fay that a number of reeds grew on that place, which, when agitated by the wind, always uttered the very words which had been buried beneath, and publifhed to the world, that Midas had the ears of an afs.   Some have endeavoured to explain the fable of the ears of Midas, by a fuppofition that he kept a number of informers and fpies, who were continually employed in gathering every feditious word which might drop from the mouths of his fubjects.

The

The favourites of Apollo were; Leucothoe, a daughter of king Orchamus: To introduce himself to her with greater facility, he assumed the shape and features of her mother ; but Clytia, who was herself in love with Apollo, prompted by jealousy, discovered the whole intrigue to the father of her rival, who caused his daughter to be buried alive. The lover, unable to save her from death, sprinkled Nectar and Ambrosia on her tomb, which penetrating to the body, changed it into a beautiful tree, which bears frankincense. Daphne, a daughter of the River Peneus, or, of the Ladon, by the Goddess Terra: The passion of Apollo for her, had been raised by Cupid, with whom the former, proud of his victory over the Serpent Python, had disputed the power of his darts. Daphne heard with horror the addresses of the God, and endeavoured to avoid his importunities by flight; Apollo pursued her, and Daphne seeing him ready to overtake her, entreated the assistance of the Gods, who immediately changed her into a laurel. Apollo afterwards crowned his head with the leaves of the laurel, and ordained that *that* tree should be for ever sacred to him. Isse, a daughter of Macareus, the son of Lycaon: Apollo, to obtain her confidence, took the form of a shepherd

o

to

to whom fhe was attached. Bolina, a virgin
of Achaia, who rejected his addreffes, and
threw herfelf into the fea to avoid his importunities. The God made her immortal. There
is a city which bears her name in Achaia.
Coronis, a daughter of Phlegias, a fon of
Mars, and king of the Lapithæ in Theffaly.
She was the mother of Efculapius, but was
killed by Apollo, before the birth of her fon,
on account of her criminal partiality to Ifchys
the Theffalian. Efculapius, however, was taken
from his mother when fhe was on the funeral
pîle, and preferved by Mercury. Cyrene, a
daughter of the River Peneus, of whom Apollo
became enamoured; he carried her to that
part of Africa which is called Cyrenaica, where
fhe brought forth Ariftæus. Chione, a daughter of Dædalion, by whom Apollo had a fon,
named Philammon, who became an excellent
mufician. Acacallis, a nymph, mother of Phi-
lander and Phylacis : they were expofed to the
wild beafts in Crete, but a goat giving them
her milk, preferved them. Calliope, one of
the Mufes, daughter of Jupiter and Mnemofyne.
She is faid to be the mother of Orpheus, by
Apollo. Perfeis, one of the Oceanides, mother of Pafiphae (who married Minos, king of
Crete), and of the forcerefs Circe. Clemene,
one

one of the Oceanides, and the mother of Phaeton : this young man was of a lively difpofition,
and a handfome figure ; he became a favourite
of Venus, who entrufted him with one of her
temples. Seeing himfelf thus diftinguifhed by
the Goddefs, he grew vain and afpiring ; and
when told by Epaphus, the fon of Io, that he
ought to check his pride, for that he was not
as he imagined, the fon of Phœbus : Phaeton
refolved to know his true origin, and, by the
advice of his mother, he vifited the palace of the
Sun. He begged Phœbus, that if he really was
his father, he would give him inconteftible
proofs of his paternal tendernefs, and convince
the world of his ligitimacy. Phœbus fwore
by the Styx, that he would grant whatever he
required; and no fooner had he pronounced
that oath, than Phaeton demanded his permiffion to drive his chariot for one day. Phœbus reprefented the impropriety of fuch a requeft, and the dangers to which it would expofe
him, but in vain; and as the oath was inviolable, and Phaeton unmoved, the father inftructed his fon how to proceed in his way through
he regions of the air. His explicit directions
were forgotten, or rather not attended to ; and
no fooner had Phaeton received the reins from
his father, than he betrayed his ignorance and
incapacity

incapacity of guiding the chariot. The flying horfes became fenfible of the confufion of their driver, and immediately departed from the ufual track. Phaeton repented too late of his rafh-nefs, and already Heaven and earth were threatened with an univerfal conflagration; when Jupiter, who had perceived the diforder of the horfes of the fun, ftruck their driver with one of his thunder-bolts, and hurled him headlong from Heaven into the river Po. His body, confumed with fire, was found by the nymphs of the place, and honoured with a decent burial. His fifters, mourning day and night his unhappy end, were at laft changed into poplars by Jupiter. According to thofe who explain this poetical fable, Phaeton was a Li-gurian Prince, who ftudied aftronomy, and in whofe age the neighbourhood of the Po was vifited with uncommon heats.

Apollo had a great affection for young Hya-cynthus, whom he killed accidentally with a quoit. He was much afflicted at this misfortune, and changed the blood of his favourite into a flower which bears his name. His body was placed among the conftellations. Cypariffus, another youth, was much beloved by Apollo. Having killed a favourite ftag of the God;
:   be

he was fo grieved at it that he pined away, and was changed by Apollo into a cyprefs tree.

Apollo is reprefented as a tall, beardlefs young man, with long hair, and a handfome fhape, holding in his hand a bow, and fometimes a lyre, which he is faid to have received from Mercury, and to have given him in return, the famous Caduceus, with which Apollo was wont to drive the flocks of king Admetus. His head is generally furrounded with beams of light, and crowned with laurel. He was the Deity, who, according to the notions of the ancients, inflicted plagues, and his power was univerfally acknowledged. He had temples and ftatues in every country, particularly in Egypt, Greece, and Italy. His ftatue, which ftood upon Mount Actium, as a mark to mariners to avoid the dangerous coaft, was particularly famous, and it was feen at a great diftance upon the fea. As he prefided over poetry, Apollo was often feen on Mount Parnaffus with the Nine Mufes. His moft famous oracles were at Delphi, Delos, Claros, Tenedos, Cyrrha, and Patara. His moft fplendid temple was at Delphi, where every nation and individual made confiderable prefents when they they confulted the oracle. Auguftus, after the

battle

battle of Actium, built a temple to this God on Mount Palatine, which he enriched with a valuable library. The famous Coloſſus at Rhodes was a ſtatue of Apollo : it was one of the Seven Wonders of the World. The cock, the graſshopper, the wolf, the crow, the ſwan, the hawk, the olive, the laurel, the palm tree, &c. were all ſacred to Apollo ; and in his ſacrifices wolves and hawks were offered, as being the natural enemies of the flocks, over which he preſided. Bullocks and lambs were alſo immolated to him. Apollo, beſides the ſir-names already mentioned, was likewiſe called Delius, Cynthius, Pæan, Delphicus, Lycius, Clarius, Iſmenius, Vulturius, Smintheus, &c.

MERCURY.

MERCURY.

———

MERCURY, the fon of Jupiter and Maia.
He was called by the Greeks, Hermes. There
was no lefs than five of this name according to
Cicero. A fon of Cœlus and Lux; a fon of
Valens and Coronis; a fon of the Nile; the
the fon of Jupiter and Maia; and another,
a great philofopher among the Egyptians, who
was called by them Hermes, and Mercurius
Trifmegiftus. To the fon of Jupiter and Maia,
the actions of all the reft have been probably
attributed, as he is the moft famous of them
all. Mercury was the meffenger of the Gods,
and of Jupiter more particularly: He was
the patron of travellers and of fhepherds. It
was his office to conduct the fouls of the dead
into the infernal regions; and he not only pre-
prefided over orators and merchants, but he
was alfo the God of Thieves, and all difho-
neft perfons. He was fuppofed to have been
born on Mount Cyllene, in Arcadia, and entrufted to the care of the Seafons. Mercury
gave

gave an early proof of his craftinefs and difho-
nefty, in ftealing the oxen of Admetus, which
Apollo 'tended.   He gave another proof of his
thievifh propenfity, by taking alfo the quiver
and arrows of the divine fhepherd ; and he in-
creafed his fame by robbing Neptune of his
trident, Venus of her girdle, Mars of his fword,
Jupiter of his fceptre, and Vulcan of many of
his mechanical inftruments.   Thefe fpecimens
of his art recommended him to the notice of
the Gods : he was their ambaffador, and was
concerned in all treaties and alliances.   As the
meffenger of Jupiter, Mercury was entrufted
with all his fecrets, and the confident of his
amours.   He was prefented by him, with a
winged cap, called *Petafus*, and with wings
for his feet, called *Talaria*.   He had alfo a
fhort fword, called *Herpe*, which he lent to
Perfeus, when that hero went to attack the Gorgons.   With thefe he was enabled to go into
whatever part of the univerfe he pleafed, with
the greateft celerity ; and he had befides the
power of becoming invifible, and of affuming
whatever fhape he thought proper.   The invention of the lyre and its feven ftrings is
afcribed to Mercury.   This he gave to Apollo, and received from him in exchange the celebrated Caduceus, which is a winged rod, en-
circled

circled by a couple of ferpents, and by means of which he was faid to poffefs the faculty of deciding controverfies, and compofing differences. From hence ambaffadors, who are fent to make peace, are called *Caduceatores*. In the wars of the giants against the Gods, Mercury shewed himfelf brave, fpirited, and active. He delivered Mars from the long confinement which he fuffered from the fuperior power of the Aloides. He purified the Danaides of the murder of their hufbands. He tied Ixion to his wheel in the infernal regions. He destroyed the hundred eyed Argus. He fold Hercules to Omphale, queen of Lydia. He conducted Priam to the tent of Achilles, to redeem the body of his fon, Hector; and he carried the infant Bacchus to the nymphs of Nyfa. When Mercury was ftealing the oxen of Admetus, he was feen by a herdfman whofe name was Battus. The God, on perceiving that his theft was difcovered, gave Battus a cow, who thereupon promifed him fecrecy; but Mercury, foon after, to prove his fidelity, came to him in another fhape, and enquired if he knew who had ftolen the oxen, and which way the thief had led them, promifing him both a bull and a cow if he fhould difcover it. Battus was unable to refift this offer, and he revealed
all

all he knew; when Mercury, enraged at this double treachery, turned Battus into a pumice ſtone.

Mercury accompanied Jupiter when he tra- velled in difguiſe over Aſia. The Gods came to a ſmall cottage where Philemon, an aged peaſant, with his wife, Baucis, lived content- ed and happy in their humble ſtation. Theſe good people received their unknown gueſts with ſuch cheerful hoſpitality, that the deities to recompence their virtue, metamorphoſed their dwelling into a magnificent temple, of which Philemon and Baucis were made prieſts. After they had lived happy to an extreme old age, they died both at the ſame hour, ac- cording to their own requeſt, that one might not have the ſorrow of ſurviving the other. Their bodies were at the ſame inſtant changed into two yew-trees before the door of the temple.

The children of Mercury were numerous, as well as his amours. He was father of Au- tolycus, by Chione; of Myrtilus, by Cleobula; of Lybys, by Lybias; of Echion and Eurytus, by Antianira; and of Prylis, by Iſſa. He was alſo father of Hermaphroditus, by Venus; of Eudorus,

Eudorus, by Polimela; of Pan, by Dryope; and of Cephalus, by Herfe, a daughter of Cecrops, king of Athens. Mercury difclofed his love for Herfe, to her fifter Aglauros, in the hope of obtaining an eafy admittance to his miftrefs by her means; but Aglauros, through jealoufy, difcovered the amour. The God was fo incensed at her behaviour, that he ftruck her with his caduceus, and changed her into a ftone.

The worfhip of Mercury was well eftablifhed; particularly in Greece, Egypt, and Italy. He was worfhiped at Tanagra in Bœotia, under the name of Criophorus, and reprefented as carrying a ram on his fhoulders; becaufe he delivered the inhabitants from a peftilence, by directing them to carry a ram in that manner round the walls of their city. The Roman merchants yearly celebrated a feftival on the fifteenth of May, in honour of Mercury, in a temple near the Circus Maximus. A pregnant fow was then facrificed, and fometimes a calf; and particularly the tongues of animals were offered to him by throwing them into the fire, as he was the patron of eloquence, of which the tongue is the organ. After the votaries had fprinkled themfelves

felves with water, with laurel. leaves, they offered prayers to the Divinity, and entreated
him to be favourable to them, and to forgive
whatever artful meafures, falfe oaths, or other
deceits they had made ufe of in the purfuit of
gain.

. Mercury fometimes appears on monuments,
with a large cloak round his arm, or tied under his chin. The chief enfigns of his power
and offices are his Caduceus, his Petafus, and
his Talaria. Sometimes he is reprefented fitting upon a cray-fifh, holding in one hand his
Caduceus, and in the other the claws of the
fifh. At other times he is feen like a young
man without a beard, holding in one hand a
purfe, as being the tutelar God of Merchants,
with a cock on his wrift, as an emblem of vigi-
lence, and at his feet a goat, a fcorpion, and
a fly. Sometimes he refts his foot upon a tortoife. In Egypt his ftatues reprefented him
with the head of a dog, whence he was often
confounded with Anubis, and received the facrifice of a ftork. Offerings of milk and
honey were made to him, becaufe he was the
God of Eloquence, whofe powers are fweet
and perfuafive. Sometimes his ftatues reprefent
him without arms, becaufe, according to fome,

the

the power of fpeech can prevail over every
thing, even without the affiftance of arms;
and fometimes to denote his fkill in making
peace, he was painted with chains of gold
flowing from his mouth, with which he linked
together the minds of thofe who heard him.

Mercury had many firnames and epithets.
He was called Cyllenius, Caduceator, Aca-
ceton, from Acacus, an Arcadian, Acacefius,
Tricephalos, Triplex, Chthonius, Camillus,
Agoneus, Delius, Arcas, &c.

MARS.

MARS.

MARS, the God of War 'amongſt the ancients, was the ſon of Jupiter and Juno, or of
Juno alone, according to Ovid, by the touch
of a flower ſhewn her by Flora, in the plains
near Olenus. The education of Mars was
entruſted by Juno to the God Priapus, who
inſtructed him in all the manly exerciſes. His
trial, before the celebrated court of the Areopagus, according to the authority of ſome authors,
for the murder of Hallirhotius (who had offered
violence to his daughter Alcippe), forms an
intereſting epocha in hiſtory. In the wars of
Jupiter and the Titans, Mars was ſeized by
Otus and Ephialtes, and confined during fifteen
months, after which Mercury procured him his
liberty. In the Trojan war, Mars intereſted
himſelf on the ſide of the Trojans, and defended the favourites of Venus with great acti-
vity. His amours with that Goddeſs have been
much celebrated. The God of War obtained
her affection ; but Vulcan being informed of
the intrigue by Apollo, made a net, of which

the workmanfhip was fo fine as to render it imperceptible. In this net he caught the two lovers, and expofed them to the ridicule and fatire of all the Gods, till Neptune prevailed upon him to fet them at liberty. This difcovery fo incenfed Mars, that he changed into a cock his favourite Alectrion, whom he had ftationed at the door of the houfe to watch the approach of the fun, and Venus alfo fhewed her refentment, by perfecuting, with the moft inveterate fury, the children of Apollo.

Mars was father of Cupid, Anteros, and Harmonia, by the goddefs Venus. He had Afcalaphus and Ialmenus, who were at the Trojan war, by Aftyoche, a daughter of Actor ; Alcippe, by Aglauros, a daughter of Cecrops ; Molus, Pylus, Evenus, and Theftius, by Demonice, the daughter of Agenor ; and Tereus, by the nymph Biftonis. Befides thefe, he was the reputed father of Romulus, OEnomaus, Bythis, Thrax, Diomedes of Thrace &c. Tereus, fon of Mars and Biftonis, was king of Thrace. He married Procne, a daughter of Pandion, king of Athens. Procne had a fifter named Philomela, whom fhe tenderly loved, and finding herfelf unhappy at being feperated from her, fhe entreated her hufband

to go to Athens, and bring her fifter to Thrace.
Tereus complied with his wife's requeft; but
he had no fooner obtained Pandion's permiffion
to conduct Philomela to his kingdom, than he
became enamoured of her, and refolved to
gratify his paffion. He difmiffed the guards
which Pandion had appointed to attend his
daughter, and conveyed her to a lonely caftle,
where he offered her violence, and afterwards
cut off her tongue, that fhe might not be able
to difcover his barbarity, and the indignities
which fhe had fuffered. He then left her confined in the caftle, and, after having taken
every precaution to prevent a difcovery, he returned to Procne, and told her, that Philomela
had died by the way, and that he had paid the
laft fad offices to her remains. Procne, at this
fad intelligence, put on mourning for the lofs of
Philomela, but a year had fcarcely elapfed, before fhe was fecretly informed that her fifter
was not dead. Philomela, during her captivity, defcribed on a piece of tapeftry her mif-
fortunes, and the brutality of Tereus, and privately conveyed it to Procne, who was going
to celebrate the orgies of Bacchus when fhe
received it. She difguifed her refentment, and,
as during the feftivals of the God of Wine fhe
was permitted to rove about the country, fhe

haftened

haſtened to deliver her ſiſter from confinement, and to concert with her how to puniſh the cruelty of Tereus. She murdered her young ſon Itylus, and ſerved him up as food before his father during the feſtival. Tereus, in the midſt of his repaſt, calling for his ſon, Procne immediately told him that he was then feaſting on his fleſh, and at the ſame inſtant Philomela appeared, and by throwing on the table the head of Itylus, convinced the monarch of the vengeance which the two ſiſters had taken on him. He drew his ſword to puniſh them both, but at the inſtant he was going to ſtab them to the heart, he was changed into a Hoopoe, Philomela into a nightingale, Procne into a ſwallow, and Itylus into a pheaſant. This tragical ſcene happened at Daulis in Phocis, but Pauſanius and Strabo, who mention the ſtory, are ſilent about the transformation, and the former obſerves, that Tereus, after this bloody repaſt, fled to Megara, where he deſtroyed himſelf. The inhabitants of the place raiſed a monument to his memory, where they offered yearly ſacrifices. It was on this monument, that the birds called Hoopoes were firſt ſeen, hence the fable of his Metamorphoſis. Procne and Philomela died through exceſs of grief and melancholy; and as the nightingale's and

the

the fwallow's voice is peculiarly plaintiff and mournful, the poets have embellifhed the fable, by fuppofing, that the two unfortunate fifters were changed into thofe birds.

Mars prefided over gladiators, and was the God of hunting, and whatever exercifes or amufements have fomething manly and warlike in them.

The worfhip of Mars was not very univerfal among the ancients. His temples were not very numerous in Greece ; but in Rome he received the moft unbounded honours, and the warlike Romans paid great homage to a Deity, whom they efteemed as the patron of their city, and the father of the firft of their monarchs. His moft celebrated temple at Rome was built by Auguftus, after the battle of Philippi. It was dedicated to Mars *Ultor*, or the avenger. His priefts among the Romans were called Salii : they were firft inftituted by Numa, and their chief office was to keep the facred Ancyle or fhield, which was fuppofed to have fallen down from heaven.

Mars was generally reprefented in the naked figure of an old man, armed with a helmet, a

C 4   pike,

pike, and a fhield. Sometimes he appeared in a military drefs, with a long flowing beard, and fometimes without. He ufually rode in a chariot drawn by furious horfes, which the poets call flight and terror, and which were conducted by Bellona, the Goddefs of War, who was by fome called the fifter of Mars, and by others his daughter, or his wife. She appears with difhevelled hair, arm'd with a whip, and carries likewife a lighted torch. The altars of Mars were ftained with the blood of the horfe, on account of his warlike fpirit, and of the wolf, on account of its voracity. Magpies and Vultures were alfo offered to him, becaufe of their greedinefs and ferocity. The Scythians generally offered him affes, and the people of Caria dogs. The weed called dog-grafs was facred to him, becaufe it grows, as it is reported, in places which are fit for fields of battle, or where the earth has been ftained with the effufion of human blood.

The firnames of Mars are not numerous. He was called Gradivus, Mavors, Quirinus, Salifubfulus, among the Romans. The Greeks called him Ares; and he was the Enyalus of the Sabines, the Camulus of the Gauls, and the Mamers of Carthage.

BACCHUS.

BACCHUS.

BACCHUS was the fon of Jupiter and Semele. The manner of his birth has been already related in the account which has been
given of the amours of Jupiter, as well as his
being carried by Mercury as foon as born to
the Nymphs of Nyfa; but there are different
traditions concerning the manner of his education. Ovid relates, that he was brought up
by his Aunt Ino, and afterwards entrufted to
the care of the Nymphs of Nyfa; and Apollonius fays, that he was carried by Mercury to a
Nymph in the Ifland of Eubœa, whence he
was driven by the power of Juno, who was
the chief Deity of the place. Some maintain
that Naxos can boaft of being the place of his
education, under the Nymphs, Philia, Coronis, and Clyda. Paufanias relates a tradition
which prevailed in the town of Brafiæ, in Peloponnefus, and accordingly mentions, that
Cadmus, the Father of Semele, fo foon as he
was informed of his daughter's amours, fhut
her up with her child, lately born, in a coffer,

and

and expofed them on the fea. The coffer was carried fafe by the waves on the coafts of Bra-fiæ; but Semele was found dead, and the child alive. Semele was honoured with a magnifi-cent funeral, and Bacchus was properly edu-cated. This diverfity of opinions fhews that there were many of the fame name. Diodo-rus fpeaks of three, and Cicero of a greater number; but among them all, the fon of Ju-piter and Semele feems to have obtained the merit of all the reft. The three perfons of the name of Bacchus, which Didorous mentions, are, the one who conquered the Indies, and who is firnamed the bearded Bacchus. A fon of Jupiter and Proferpine, who is reprefented with horns; and the fon of Jupiter and Semele, called the Bacchus of Thebes. Thofe men-tioned by Cicero, are a fon of Proferpine, a fon of Nilus, who built Nyfa; a fon of Caprius, who reigned in the Indies; a fon of Jupiter and the Moon; and a fon of Thyone and Ni-fus. Bacchus is the Ofiris of the Egyptians, and his ftory is taken from the Egyptian tradi-tions concerning that ancient king, Bacchus, who affifted the Gods in their wars againft the giants, and was cut to pieces; but the fon of Semele was not then born. This tradition therefore is taken from the Hiftory of Ofiris, who

who was killed by his brother, Typhon; and the worſhip of Oſiris was introduced by Orpheus into Greece, under the name of Bacchus.

Bacchus, in his youth, was taken aſleep in the iſland of Naxos, and carried away by ſome mariners. The God, to puniſh their temerity, transformed them all into dolphins, except the Pilot, who had expreſſed ſome concern at his misfortune. His expedition into the Eaſt is celebrated. He marched at the head of an army compoſed of women, as well as of men, all inſpired with a divine fury, and armed with Thyrſuſes, Cymbals, and other muſical inſtruments. The leader was drawn in a chariot by a lion, and a Tyger; and was accompanied by Pan, Silenus, and all the Satyrs. His conqueſts were eaſy and without bloodſhed. The people readily ſubmitted, and gratefully elevated to the rank of a God, the Hero who taught them the uſe of the vine, the cultivation of the earth, and the manner of making honey. But Bacchus, notwithſtanding his benevolence to mankind, was relentleſs in puniſhing all want of reſpect to his divinity, and the vengeance which he took on Pentheus, King of Thebes, and on Lycurgus, King of Thrace, ought not to be omitted. Pentheus

C 6

refuſed

refufed to acknowledge the divinity of Bacchus.
and even forbade his fubjects to pay adoration to
that God ; and when the Theban women had
gone of the City, to celebrate the Orgies of Bacchus, Pentheus, apprized of the debauchery
which attended this folemnity, ordered the God
himfelf, who conducted the religious multitude,
to be feized : his orders were obeyed with reluctance ; but, when the doors of the prifon, in
which Bacchus had been confined, opened of
their own accord, Pentheus became more irritated, and commanded his foldiers to deftroy the
whole band of Bacchanals : this, however,
was not executed, for Bacchus infpired the
Monarch with an ardent defire of feeing the
celebration of the Orgies. Accordingly, he
hid himfelf in a wood on Mount Citheron,
from whence he could fee all the ceremonies.
But here his curiofity foon proved fatal to
him ; he was perceived by the Bacchanals, and
they all rufhed upon him. His mother was
the firft who attacked him, and her example
was inftantly followed by her two fifters, Ino
and Autonoe, and his body was torn to pieces.
Lycurgus, according to the Mythologifts, drove
Bacchus out of his territories, and abolifhed
his worfhip, for which impiety he was feverely
punifhed by the God. He put his own fon

Dryas

Dryas to death in a fit of frenzy, and he afterwards cut off his own legs, miftaking them
for vine-boughs. He was put to death by his
own fubjects, who had been informed by an
oracle, that they fhould not tafte wine till Lycurgus was no more. This fable is explained
by obferving that the averfion of Lycurgus for
wine, over which Bacchus prefided, arofe from
the filthinefs and difgrace of intoxication, and
therefore the Monarch wifely ordered all the
vines of his dominions to be cut off, that himfelf and his fubjects might be preferved from
the extravagance and debauchery which is produced by too free an ufe of wine.   Another in-
ftance of the feverity of Bacchus, to thofe who
neglected his worfhip, may be found in the example of the three daughters of Minyas, king
of Boeotia; who defpifing the facrifices of this
God, and ftaying at home fpinning, while the
Orgies were celebrating, were changed into
bats.

Bacchus went down to Hell to recover his
mother, whom Jupiter made a Goddefs, under
the name of Thyone.

The ftory of Midas, King of Phrygia, who
has already been mentioned under the article of
Apollo,

Apollo, muſt here find a place. The hoſpitality with which he had treated Silenus, the Preceptor of Bacchus, was liberally rewarded by the God, who permitted him to chuſe whatever recompence he pleaſed. Midas had the imprudence, and the avarice, to demand, that whatever he touched might be turned into gold. His prayer was granted, but he was ſoon convinced of his injudicious choice ; and when the very meats which he attempted to eat, became gold in his mouth, he begged of Bacchus to reſume a gift, which muſt otherwiſe prove ſo fatal to him on whom it had been beſtowed. He was ordered to waſh himſelf in the river Pactolus, whoſe ſands were converted into gold by the touch of Midas.

The amours of Bacchus were not numerous. He married Ariadne, after ſhe had been forſaken by Theſeus in the iſland of Naxos, and had by her many children ; among whom were Ceranaus, Thoas, Œnopion, Tauropolis, &c. According to ſome, he was the father of Hymenæus, whom the Athenians made the God of marriage.

As Bacchus was the God of Wine and of Drinking, he is generally repreſented crowned

with

with vine and ivy leaves, with a Thyrfus in his
hand. His figure is fometimes that of an ef-
feminate young man, to denote the joys which
commonly prevail at feafts, and fometimes that
of an old man ; to teach us that wine taken im-
moderately, will enervate us, impair our health,
render us loquacious, and childifh like old men,
and unable to keep fecrets. Bacchus is fometimes reprefented like an infant, holding a
Thyrfus and clufters of Grapes, with a horn.
He often appears naked, and riding upon the
fhoulders of Pan, or in the arms of Silenus,
who was his fofter-father. He alfo fits upon
a celeftial globe, befpangled with ftars, and is
then the fame as the fun, or Ofiris of Egypt.
According to Pliny, he was the firft who ever
wore a crown. His beauty is compared to that
of Apollo, and like him he is reprefented with
fine hair, loofely flowing down his fhoulders,
and is faid to poffefs eternal youth. Sometimes
he has horns, either becaufe he firft taught the
cultivation of the earth with oxen, or becaufe
Jupiter was faid to have appeared to him in the
defarts of Libya, under the fhape of a Ram,
and to have fupplied his thirfty army with water. The feftivals of Bacchus, generally called Orgies, Bacchanalia, or Dionyfia, were introduced into Greece, from Egypt, by Danaus,

and

and his daughters. The infamous debaucheries which aroʻe froⁿ the celebration of thefe feftivals are well known. The Egyptians facrificed pigs to Bacchus, before the doors of their houfes, and the goat was generally facrificed to him, on account of the great propenfity of that animal to deftroy the vine. The Panther is facred to him, becaufe in his Indian expedition, he was covered with the fkin of that beaft. The magpie was his favourite bird, becaufe in triumphs, people were permitted to fpeak with boldnefs and liberty. The fir-tree, the yew-tree, the fig-tree, the ivy, and the vine, were all facred to him.

Among the feveral names which Bacchus has received, he is called Liber, Bromius, Lycœus, Evan, Thyonæus, Pfilas, &c. which are moftly derived from the places where he received adoration, or from the ceremonies obferved in his feftivals.

CUPID.

CUPID.

CUPID was a celebrated Deity among the Antients, God of Love, and Love itſelf. There are are different traditions concerning his parents. Cicero mentions three Cupids; one, ſon of Mercury and Diana; another, ſon of Mercury and Venus; and the third, ſon of Mars and Venus. Plato mentions two. Heſiod, the moſt antient Theogoniſt, ſpeaks only of one, who, as he ſays, was produced at the ſame time as Chaos and the Earth. There are, according to more received opinions, two Cupids, one of which is a lively ingenuous youth, ſon of Jupiter and Venus; whilſt the other, ſon of Nox and Erebus, is diſtinguiſhed by his debauchery and riotous diſpoſition. Cupid is repreſented as a winged infant, naked, with a fillet over his eyes, and armed with a bow and a quiver full of arrows. On gems, and all other pieces of antiquity, he is repreſented as amuſing himſelf with ſome childiſh diverſion. Sometimes he appears driving a hoop, throwing a quoit, playing with a Nymph, catching a butterfly, or trying to burn with a torch:

torch : at other times he plays upon a horn before his mother, or clofely embraces a fwan, or
with one foot raifed in the air, he in an amufing
pofture, feems meditating fome trick. Sometimes, like a conqueror, he marches triumphant-
ly with a helmet on his head, a fpear on his
fhoulder, and a buckler on his arm ; to intimate that even Mars himfelf owns the fupe-
riority of Love.   His power was generally expreffed by his riding upon the back of a lion,
or on a dolphin, or by breaking to pieces the
thunder-bolts of Jupiter.   Cupid was worfhipped with the fame folemnity as his mother
Venus ; and as his influence was extended over
the heavens, the fea, and the earth, and even
the empire of Pluto, his divinity was univerfally
acknowledged, and vows, prayers, and facrifices, were daily offered to him.   According to
fome accounts, the union of Cupid with Chaos
gave birth to men, and all the animals which
inhabited the earth, and even the Gods themfelves, are the offspring of Love, before the
foundation of the world.

Cupid is faid by fome to have married the
Nymph Pfyche, and to have carried her into a
place of blifs, where he long enjoyed her company.   Venus put her to death becaufe fhe had
                                        robbed

robbed the world of her fon, but Jupiter, at the requeft of Cupid granted immortality to Pfyche. The word fignifies the foul, and this perfonification of Pfyche is pofterior to the Auguftin age, though ftill it is connected with ancient Mythology.

CELESTIAL

CELESTIAL GODDESSES.

JUNO	LATONA
MINERVA	DIANA
VENUS	AURORA.

JUNO.

JUNO, as has been already obferved, was
the daughter of Saturn and Ops, and the
fifter and wife of Jupiter.   She was born at
Argos ; or, according to others, at Samos, and
was entrufted with the care of the Seafons ; or,
as Homer and Ovid mention, to Oceanus and
Thetis.   Some of the inhabitants of Argolis,
fuppofed fhe had been brought up by the Three
Daughters of the River Afterion ; and the
people of Stympholus, in Arcadia, maintained
that fhe had been educated under the care of
Temenus the fon of Pelafgus.   Jupiter was not
infenfible to the charms of his fifter ; and the
more powerfully to engage her confidence, he
changed himfelf into a cuckoo, and raifing a
great ftorm, made the air uncommonly chill
and cold ; under this form he flew to the Goddefs all fhivering.   Juno pitied the cuckoo, and
took him into her bofom.   The nuptials of
Jupiter and Juno were celebrated with the
greateft folemnity.   The Gods, all mankind,
and all the brute creation, attended.   Chelone,
a young maid, was the only one who refufed to
be

be prefent, and who derided the ceremony.
For this impiety, Mercury changed her into a
tortoife, and condemned her to perpetual filence,
from which circumftance the tortoife has always been ufed as the fymbol of filence among
the ancients. By her marriage with Jupiter,
Juno became the queen of all the Gods, and
miftrefs of Heaven and Earth. Her conjugal
happinefs, however, was frequently difturbed
by the numerous amours of her hufband, and
fhe fhewed herfelf jealous and inexorable in the
higheft degree. Her feverity to the miftreffes
and illegitimate children of Jupiter, was unpa-
ralleled. She perfecuted Hercules and his defcendants with the moft inveterate fury; and
her refentment agaiaft Paris, who had given
the golden apple to Venus, in preference to herfelf, was the caufe of the Trojan war, and of
all the miferies which overwhelmed the unfortunate houfe of Priam. Her feverities to Latona, Io, and Semele, have been already taken
notice of. Thofe which fhe exercifed upon
Ino, the daughter of Cadmus, and her two
fons, Learchus and Melicerta, were alfo remarkable. Their crime was being defcended from
Venus, whom fhe hated. The Goddefs fent
Tifiphone, one of the Furies, to the houfe of
Athamas, king of Thebes, who was the hufband
of Ino, and fhe inflamed him with fuch fudden
fury,

fury, that he took Ino to be a lionefs, and her
children to be two whelps. In this fit of madnefs, he fnatched Learchus from the arms of
his mother, and killed him, by dafhing him
againft a wall; upon which Ino fled, and with
Melicerta in her arms, threw herfelf headlong
from a high rock into the fea. Neptune, who
pitied her fate, transformed her into a Sea-
Deity, afterwards called Leucothoe. Melicerta
became alfo a Sea-God, known by the name
of Palaemon. The repeated infidelities of Jupiter at laft provoked Juno to fuch a degree,
that fhe retired to Euboea, and refolved to fee
him no more; but Jupiter procured a reconciliation by means of the following ftratagem.
The God, anxious for her return, went to
confult Cithæron, king of Platæa, to find fome
effectual means to break her obftinacy. Cithæron advifed him to drefs a ftatue in woman's
apparel, to carry it with him in a chariot, and
publicly to report it was Platæa, the daughter
of Afopus, whom he was going to marry. The
advice was followed, and Juno being informed
of her hufband's intended marriage, repaired in
hafte to meet the chariot, when difcovering the
contrivance that had been made ufe of, fhe was
eafily prevailed upon to forgive, and be re-united
to Jupiter. But this reconciliation, however

cordial

cordial it might appear, was soon diſſolved by new offences; and to ſilence the complaints of the jealous Goddeſs, Jupiter had ſometimes recourſe to violent meaſures. He even puniſhed the cruelties which ſhe had exerciſed upon his ſon Hercules, by ſuſpending her from the heavens by a golden chain, and faſtening a heavy anvil to her feet. Vulcan was puniſhed for aſſiſting his mother in this degrading ſituation; Jupiter kicked him down from heaven, and he broke his leg in the fall. This puniſhment rather irritated than reclaimed Juno. She reſolved to revenge it, and engaged ſome of the Gods to conſpire againſt Jupiter; but Thetis delivered him from this conſpiracy, by bringing to his aſſiſtance the famous Briareus. Apollo and Neptune were baniſhed from heaven for joining in the conſpiracy, though ſome attribute their exile to different cauſes.

Juno brought Jupiter ſome children, according to Heſiod ſhe was mother of Mars, Hebe, Ilithyia, or Lucina, and Vulcan; and from him we have it, that it was this laſt, and not Mars, whom ſhe conceived by the touch, or ſmell of a certain plant or flower. According to others, it was neither Mars nor Vulcan, but Hebe that ſhe brought forth in this manner, and they

D relate

relate that it was after eating some lettuces at
the table of Apollo.

The worſhip of Juno was univerſal, and even
more ſo than that of Jupiter, according to
ſome authors.   Her ſacrifices were offered with
the greateſt ſolemnity.   She was particularly
worſhipped at Argos, Samos, Carthage, and
afterwards at Rome.   Her temples were numerous; the moſt famous of which were at
Argos, Olympia, &c.   At Rome no woman
of bad character was permitted to enter her
temple, or even to touch it.   Juno protected
cleanlineſs, and preſided over marriage and
child-birth.   She particularly patronized the
moſt faithful and virtuous of the ſex, and ſe-
verely puniſhed incontinence in matrons.   She
was the Goddeſs of all power and empire, and
the patroneſs of riches.   The ancients generally offered on her altars an ewe-lamb and a
ſow, the firſt day of every month.   No cows
were ever immolated to her, becauſe ſhe aſ-
ſumed the nature of that animal when the Gods
fled into Egypt in their war with the Giants.
Among the birds, the hawk, the gooſe, and
particularly the peacock were ſacred to her.
The dittany, the poppy, and the lilly were her
favourite flowers; the latter was ſaid to have
been

been originally of the colour of the crocus; but Jupiter having placed Hercules, when an infant, at the breaſt of Juno while ſhe was aſleep, ſome of her milk fell down upon the earth, and changed the colour of the lillies from purple to a beautiful white. Some of the milk alſo dropped in that part of the heavens, which, from its whiteneſs, ſtill retains the name of the Milky Way. As Juno's power was extended over all the Gods, ſhe often made uſe of the Godeſs Minerva as her meſſenger, and even had the privilege of hurling the thunder of Jupiter when ſhe pleaſed. She is repreſented ſitting on a throne, with a diadem on her head, and a golden ſceptre in her right hand. Some peacocks generally ſit by her, and a cuckoo is often perched on her ſceptre, while Iris behind her, diſplays the thouſand colours of her beautiful rainbow. She is ſometimes carried through the air in a rich chariot, drawn by peacocks. The Roman conſuls, when they entered upon office, were always obliged to offer her a ſolemn ſacrifice. The Juno of the Romans was called Romana, or Matrona. She was generally repreſented as veiled from head to foot, and the Roman matrons always imitated this manner of dreſſing, and deemed

D 2   it

it indecent in a married woman to leave any part of her body, except her face, uncovered.

. The firnames of Juno are various; they are derived either from the functions, or things over which fhe prefided, or from the places where her worfhip was eftablifhed. She is called Saturnia, Olympia, Samia, Argiva, Lacedæmonia, Telchinia, Candrena, Refcinthes, Profymna, Imbrafia, Acrea, Citheronia, Bunea, Ammonia, Fluonia, Anthea, Migale, Gemelia, Tropeia, Boopis, Parthenos, Teleia, Xera, Egophage, Hyperchinia, Juga, Ilithyia, Lucina, Pronuba, Caprotina, Mena, Populonia, Lacinia, Sofpita, Moneta, Curis, Domiduca, Februa, Opigenia, &c.

IRIS.

—

THIS attendant of Juno was a daughter of Thaumas and Electra, one of the Oceanides. She was the meffenger of the Gods, and more particularly of Juno. It was her office to cut the thread, which feemed to detain the foul in the body of thofe who were expiring.

She

She is the fame as the rainbow, and from that circumftance, is reprefented with all the variegated colours of that beautiful meteor, and fhe appears behind Juno ready to execute her commands. To denote her fwiftnefs, fhe is painted with wings, and is fometimes feen riding on a rainbow.

MINERVA.

MINERVA.

MINERVA, the Goddefs of Wifdom, War, and of all the liberal arts, was produced from Jupiter's brain without a mother. The God, as it is reported, had married Metis, whofe fuperior prudence and fagacity above the reft of the Gods, made him apprehend, that the off-fpring of fuch an union would be of a more exalted nature, and more intelligent than their father. To prevent this, Jupiter devour'd Metis in her pregnancy, and fometime after, to relieve the pains which he fuffered in his head, he ordered Vulcan to cleave it open, when Minerva fprung, all armed, and grown up from his brain. She was immediately admitted into the affembly of the Gods, and proved one of the moft faithful counfellors of her father. The power of Minerva was great in heaven. She could hurl the thunders of Jupiter, prolong the lives of men, beftow the gift of prophecy; and, indeed, fhe was the only one of all the Divinities, whofe authority and confequence were equal to thofe of Jupiter. The actions

of

of this Goddefs are numerous, as well as the
kindnefles by which fhe endeared herfelf to
mankind. Her quarrel with Neptune, concerning the right of giving a name to the capital of Cecropia, deferves attention. The affembly of the Gods fettled the difpute, by promifing the preference to whoever of the two
gave the moft ufeful prefent to the inhabitants.
Neptune then ftruck the earth with his trident,
and immediately a horfe iffued from it. Minerva
produced the olive, and obtained the victory by
the unanimous voice of the Gods, who obferved,
that the olive, which is the emblem of peace, is
far preferable to the horfe, which is the fymbol
of war and bloodfhed. The victorious Deity
called the capital Athenæ, and became the tutelary Goddefs of the place. Minerva was alfo
extremely jealous of her power, of which the
punifhment fhe inflicted on the prefumptuous
Arachne is a proof. Arachne was the daughter of a dyer of Colophon : fhe was fo fkilful
in embroidery, that fhe challenged Minerva,
the Goddefs of the Art, to a trial of fkill. She
reprefented on her work, the amours of Jupiter
with Europa, Antiope, Leda, Afteria, Danae,
Alcmena, &c. but though her piece was perfect and mafterly, fhe was defeated by the Goddefs, and hanging herfelf in defpair, was changed

D 4   into

into a fpider by Minerva. Some relate that Tirefias was deprived of his fight by Minerva, becaufe he had feen her bathing in the fountain of Helicon; but he obtained from the Goddefs, as fome alleviation of his misfortune, the gift of prophecy. She likewife gave him a ftaff, which conducted his fteps with as much fafety as if he had ftill enjoyed the ufe of his eye-fight.

Ovid affigns a different caufe for the blind-nefs of Tirefias, and fays, that Jupiter and Juno, in a difpute which they had, made him judge. The queftion was, which of the two fexes enjoyed the greateft fhare of happinefs. Tirefias was well qualified to pronounce on it, becaufe, having once killed a fhe-ferpent, he had thereupon been transformed into a woman, and feven years after, when he killed a he-ferpent, he had recovered his original fex. He pronounced in favour of Jupiter, who had maintained that the female fex was the happieft, and Juno, for this decifion, punifhed Tirefias, by depriving him of his fight.

The refiftance which Minerva oppofed to the violence offered her by Vulcan, is a proof of her virtue. Jupiter had fworn by the Styx, to

grant

grant to Vulcan (who had made him a complete fuit of armour) whatever he defired.
Vulcan demanded Minerva in marriage, and
the father of the Gods, who had permitted her
to live in perpetual celibacy, yet confented on
account of his oath, but privately advifed his
daughter to make ufe of every effort to fruftrate
the attempts of her lover; accordingly both
the prayers and force of Vulcan proved inef-
fectual, and the Goddefs preferved her chaftity
inviolate. Minerva was the firft who built a
fhip; and it was her zeal for navigation, and her
care for the Argonauts, which placed the prophetic tree of Dodona behind the fhip Argo
when going to Colchis. This Goddefs exerted
herfelf ftrongly on the fide of the Greeks, at the
fiege of Troy, and protected her favourite
hero Ulyffes, through all the dangers which he
encountered in his return to his kingdom.

The worfhip of Minerva was univerfally
eftablifhed. She had magnificent temples in
Egypt, Phœnicia, all parts of Greece, Italy,
Gaul, and Sicily. Sais, Rhodes, and Athens,
particularly claimed her attention. It was even
faid that Jupiter rained a fhower of gold upon
the ifland of Rhodes, which had paid fo much
veneration, and fuch an early reverence to the

divinity

divinity of his daughter. The feftivals celebrated in honour of Minerva were folemn and
magnificent. She was invoked by every artift,
and particularly by fuch as worked in wool,
embroidery, painting, and fculpture. Almoft
every meinber of fociety thought it a duty to
implore the affiftance and patronage of a Deity
who prefided over fenfe, tafte, and reafon.

Minerva was reprefented in different ways,
according to the different characters in which
fhe appeared. She had ufually a countenance
more expreffive of mafculine firmnefs and compofure, than of foftnefs and grace. She was
moft frequently reprefented with a helmet on
her head, with a large plume waving in the air;
in one hand fhe held a fpear, and in the other a
fhield, with the head of Medufa upon it : this
fhield was called the Ægis. Sometimes the
head of Medufa was feen on the breaft-plate of
the Goddefs, with living fnakes writhing round
it, as well as on her fhield and helmet. Medufa
was one of the three Gorgons, daughters of
Phorcys and Ceto. She was faid to be the only
one of the three who was fubject to mortality.
She is celebrated for her perfonal charms, and
particularly for the beauty of her hair; but
having liftened to the paffion which Neptune
had

had for her, in the temple of Minerva, the Goddefs was fo incenfed at this violation of the fanctity, of her temple, that fhe changed the beautiful locks of Medufa, which had infpired Neptune's love, into ferpents. According to Apollodorus and others, Medufa and her fifters came into the world with fnakes on their heads inftead of hair, with yellow wings and brazen hands ; their bodies were alfo covered with impenetrable fcales, and their very looks had the power of killing, or turning to ftones thofe who were fo unfortunate as to meet them. Perfeus rendered his name immortal by the conqueft of Medufa ; he cut off her head, and placed it on the Ægis of Minerva, which he had ufed in his expedition. The head ftill retained the fame petrifying power as before.

In moft of her ftatues, Minerva is reprefented as fitting, and fometimes fhe holds in one hand a diftaff inftead of a fpear. When fhe appears as the Goddefs of the Liberal Arts, fhe is arrayed in a variegated veil, which the Ancients called *Peplum*. Sometimes Minerva's helmet was covered at the top with the figure of a cock ; a bird which, on account of his great courage, is properly facred to the Goddefs of War. Some of her ftatues reprefent her helmet with a

fphinx

sphinx in the middle, supported on either side
by griffins. In some medals, a chariot drawn
by four horses, and sometimes by a dragon, or
a serpent with winding spires, appears at the
top of her helmet. The Palladium was a celebrated statue of this Goddess; it was about
three cubits high, and represented her as sitting,
and holding a pike in her right hand, and in
her left a distaff and a spindle. It was said to
have fallen down from Heaven near the tent
of Ilus, when that Prince was building the
citadel of Ilium. Some, however, suppose
that it fell at Pessinus, in Phrygia; or, according to others, Dardanus received it as a
present from his mother Electra. There are
some authors, who maintain that the Palladium
was made of the bones of Pelops, by Abaris;
but Apollodorus seems to say, that it was no
more than a piece of clockwork, which moved
of itself. However discordant the opinions of
ancient authors may be concerning this famous
statue, it is universally agreed, that on its preservation depended the safety of Troy. This
fatality was well known to the Greeks during
the Trojan war, and therefore Ulysses and
Diomedes were commissioned to steal it away.
They effected their purpose, and, if we rely
upon the authority of some authors, they were
directed

directed how to carry it away by Helenus, the
son of Priam, who proved in this unfaithful to
his country, becaufe his brother Deiphobus, at
the death of Paris, had married Helen, of
whom he was enamoured. Minerva was dif-
pleafed with the violence which was offered to
her ftatue, and, according to Virgil, the Palladium itfelf appeared to have received life and
motion; and by the flafhes which ftarted from
its eyes, and its fudden fprings from the earth,
it feemed to fhew the refentment of the Goddefs.
The true Palladium, as fome authors obferve,
was not carried away from Troy by the Greeks,
but only one of the ftatues of fimilar fize and
fhape, which were placed near it, to deceive
whatever facrilegious *perfons* attempted to fteal it.
The Palladium, therefore, as they fay, was
conveyed fafe from Troy to Italy by Æneas,
and it was afterwards preferved by the Romans
with the greateft fecrecy and veneration, in the
temple of Vefta, a circumftance which none
but the veftal virgins knew.

Minerva was partial to the olive-tree. The
owl, as well as the cock, was her favourite
among the birds, and the dragon among rep-
tiles, was facred to her. The functions, offices, and actions, attributed to this Goddefs,

feem

seem fo numerous, that they muſt have ori-
ginated in more than one perſon. Cicero
ſpeaks of five perſons of the name; a Minerva,
mother of Apollo; a daughter of the Nile, who
was worſhipped at Sais, in Egypt; a third, born
from Jupiter's brains; a fourth, daughter of
Jupiter and Corophe; and a fifth, daughter of
Pallas, generally repreſented with winged ſhoes.
Minerva was called Athena, from the city of
Athens, of which, as it hath been related, ſhe
was the tutelary Deity, and Pallas, from the
giant of that name, whom ſhe killed; Parthenos, from her remaining in perpetual celi-
bācy; Tritonia, becauſe worſhipped near the
lake Tritonis; Glaucopis, from the blueneſs
of her eyes; Agoria from her preſiding over
markets; Hippia, becauſe ſhe firſt taught
mankind how to manage the horſe; Stratea
and Area, from her martial character; Cory-
phagenes, becauſe born of Jupiter's brains; Sais,
becauſe worſhipped at Sais, &c. Some attribute to her the invention of the flute, whence
ſhe was ſirnamed Andon, Luſcinia, Muſica,
Salpiga, &c. It is ſaid, that as ſhe once
amuſed herſelf in playing upon this inſtru-
ment before Juno and Venus, thoſe Goddeſſes
ridiculed the diſtortion of her features which
it occaſioned. Minerva was afterwards convinced

vinced of the juftice of their remarks, by looking at herfelf in a fountain near mount Ida while fhe was blowing the flute. She immediately threw it away, and denounced a melancholy fate to whoever fhould find it. Marfyas was the miferable proof of the veracity of her pre-diction.

VENUS.

VENUS.

VENUS was one of the moſt celebrated Deities among the Ancients; ſhe was the Goddeſs of Beauty, the Mother of Love, the Queen of Pleaſures, and the Miſtreſs of the Graces. Some Mythologiſts ſpeak of more than one Venus. Plato mentions two; Venus Urania, the daughter of Uranus, and Venus Popularia, the daughter of Jupiter and Dione. Cicero ſpeaks of four; a daughter of Cœlus and Light, one ſprung from the froth of the ſea, a third daughter of Jupiter and the Nereid Dione, and a fourth born at Tyr, and the ſame as the Aſtarte of the Syrians. Of all theſe, however, the Venus ſprung from the froth of the ſea is moſt known, and of her in particular, ancient Mythologiſts take notice; ſhe was ſaid to ariſe from the ſea, near the Iſland of Cyprus, or according to Heſiod, of Cythera, whither ſhe was wafted by the Zephirs, and received on the ſhore by the Seaſons, daughters of Jupiter and Themis. She was ſoon after carried to Heaven, where all the Gods were ſtruck with her beauty, and all

the

the Goddeffes became jealous of her fuperior at-
tractions. Jupiter himfelf attempted to gain
her affections, but Venus rejected his fuit, and
the God, to punifh her obftinacy ; gave her in
marriage to his ugly and deformed fon Vulcan.
This marriage did not prevent the Goddefs of
Love from purfuing her own inclinations, and
fhe difhonoured her hufband by her amours with
the other gods. Her intrigue with Mars has
been already related ; by him fhe became Mother of Hermoine or Harmonia, Cupid, and
Anteros. By Mercury fhe had Hermaphroditus ; by Bacchus, Priapus ; and by Neptune,
Eryx. Her partiality for Adonis made her
abandon the feats of Olympus. Adonis was a
moft beautiful youth, the fon of Cinyras, by his
daughter Myrrha : he received a mortal wound
from a wild boar, which he had pierced, and
Venus, after fhedding many tears at his death,
changed him into a flower, called Anemona.
Proferpine is faid to have reftored him to life, on
condition that he fhould fpend fix months with
her, and the reft of the year with Venus ; this
implies the alternate return of fummer and win-
ter. Adonis is frequently taken for Ofiris,
becaufe the feftivals of both were often begun
with mournful lamentations, and finifhed with
a revival of joy, as if they were returning to
life

life again. Adonis had temples raifed to his
memory, and is faid to have been likewife the
favourite both of Apollo and Bacchus. Anchifes, a fon of Capys by Themis, was alfo beloved
by Venus, and for his fake, fhe often vifited the
woods and folitary retreats of Mount Ida. By
him fhe had Eneas ; who when Troy was taken
carried his father, then old and infirm, upon his
fhoulders, through the flames, and thus faved
his life. Anchifes accompanied his fon in his
voyage towards Italy, and died in Sicily.

The power of Venus over the heart, was
fupported and affifted by a celebrated girdle,
called Zone by the Greeks, and Ceftus by the
Latins. This myfterious girdle gave beauty,
grace, and elegance when worn even by the
moft deformed. It excited love, and rekindled extinguifhed flames. Juno herfelf was
indebted to this famous ornament, to regain the
favour of Jupiter, and Venus herfelf, though
poffeffed of every charm, found it ufeful ; fhe
no fooner put on her ceftus, than Vulcan, unable to refift its influence, forgot all the infidelities of his wife ; and, at her requeft, fabricated arms even for her illegitimate children.

The

The conteſt of Venus, for the golden apple, is well known; ſhe gained the prize from Pallas and Juno, and rewarded Paris; their Judge, with the love of the beautiful and dangerous Helen. The conſequence of this judgment was the Trojan war, of which I ſhall here proceed to give ſome account. Paris was a ſon of Priam, King of Troy; he was deſtined, even before his birth, to become the ruin of his country, and when his mother Hecuba, during her pregnancy, dreamed that ſhe ſhould bring forth a torch, which would ſet fire to her palace, the ſoothſayers foretold the calamities which might be expected from the imprudence of her future ſon, and which would end in the deſtruction of Troy. Priam, to prevent ſo great an evil, ordered a ſlave to deſtroy the child as ſoon as born. The ſlave, either touched with compaſſion, or influenced by Hecuba, did not deſtroy him; but was ſatisfied to expoſe him on Mount Ida, where the ſhepherds of the place found and educated him. Paris, though brought up among peaſants, gave early proofs of courage and intrepidity; and from his care in protecting the flocks from the rapacity of wild beaſts, he obtained the name of Alexander (helper or defender). He married the Nymph Œnone, with whom he lived in the moſt perfect

fect tendernefs, but their conjugal peace was foon difturbed. At the marriage of Peleus and Thetis, the Goddefs of difcord, who had not been invited to the entertainment, fhewed her difpleafure by throwing into the affembly of the Gods, who were at the celebration of the nuptials, a golden apple, on which were written thefe words, *Let the faireft take it.* All the Goddeffes claimed it, each as her right, and the contention at firft was general, but all the others foon yielded up their pretenfions, and only three, Juno, Venus, and Minerva continued to difpute their title to the prize of beauty. The Gods unwilling to become arbiters in an affair of fo tender and delicate a nature, appointed Paris to adjudge the prize ; and indeed the fhepherd feemed properly qualified to decide fo great a conteft, his prudence and fagacity were fo well known. The Goddeffes appeared before their judge, without any ornament, and each tried by promifes and entreaties, to gain his attention, and influence his judgment: Juno promifed him a kingdom, Minerva military glory, and Venus, the faireft woman in the world for his wife. After he had heard their feveral claims and promifes, Paris adjudged the prize to Venus, and gave her the golden apple, to which, perhaps, fhe was alfo

entitled

entitled as Goddefs of Beauty. But this decifion in her favour, drew upon the judge, and his family, the refentment of the other two Goddefles. Soon after, Priam propofed a conteft among his fons and other princes, and promifed to reward the conqueror with one of the fineft bulls of Mount Ida; he fent to procure the animal, and it was found in the poffeffion of Paris, who reluctantly yielded it up; but being defirous of recovering this favourite animal, he went himfelf to Troy, and entered the lifts as one of the combatants. The unknown Prince obtained the victory over all his rivals; even Hector himfelf, the moft valiant and famous of all the fons of Priam, was obliged to yield the prize to him; but enraged to fee himfelf thus defeated, by an obfcure ftranger, he purfued Paris, who muft have fallen a victim to his brother's refentment, had not his fifter Caffandra interpofed, and faved him from the effects of it. This princefs, who was poffeffed of uncommon penetration, and, as fome pretend, of the gift of prophecy, had been ftruck with the refemblance which the young ftranger bore to her own family: fhe enquired minutely into every circumftance, relative to his birth and age, and having difcovered that he was her brother, fhe prefented him to Priam, who for-

getful

getful of the omens which had influenced him to meditate his death, immediately acknowledged Paris as his fon, and all jealoufy ceafed among the brothers. Paris now remembered the promife made him by the Goddefs of beauty. The tranfcendant charms of Helena, the daughter of Jupiter and Leda (reputed the daughter of Tyndarus), were talked of, both in Greece and Afia, fhe was univerfally allowed to be the faireft of her fex, and Paris believed himfelf to be entitled to her (though fhe was already the wife of Menelaus, King of Sparta), and he refolved to obtain her. He equipped a fleet, and not daring to avow his purpofe, he gave out that this expedition was to recover Hefione, his father's fifter, whom Hercules had carried away, and obliged to marry Telamon the fon of Æcus. Paris departed, and foon after arrived at the Court of Sparta, where he was kindly received, and during the abfence of Menelaus in Crete, he perfuaded Helen to elope with him, and to fly to Afia; fhe confented, and Priam received her into his palace without difficulty, being pleafed with this opportunity of revenging on the Greeks the infult offered to his fifter, and her detention in their country. When Menelaus had married Helen, all her fuitors, who were very nu-

merous, had engaged themselves by a solemn
oath to protect her person, and to defend her
from every violence; the injured husband,
therefore, now reminded them of that engagement, and called upon them to recover Helen.
All Greece united in the cause of Menelaus,
and every Prince furnished a certain number of
ships and soldiers. According to Euripides,
Virgil, and Lycophron, the armament of the
Greeks amounted to 1000 ships. Homer mentions them as being 1186, and Thucydides
supposes that they were 1200. The number of
men which these ships carried, is not ascer-
tained; yet as the largest contained about 120
men each, and the smallest about 50, it may
be supposed that no less than 100,000 men were
engaged in this celebrated expedition. Agamemnon King of Mycenæ and Argos, the brother of Menelaus, was chosen General of all
these forces, but the Kings and Princes of
Greece were admitted among his Counsellors,
and by them all the operations of the war were
directed. The most celebrated of the Grecian
Princes who distinguished themselves in this
war, were Achilles, Ajax, Menelaus, Ulysses,
Diomedes, Protesilaus, Patroclus, Agamemnon, Neoptolemus, &c. The Grecian army
was opposed by a more numerous force. The
King

king of Troy received affiftance from the neighbouring Princes in Afia Minor, and reckoned
among his moft active Generals, Rhefus, king
of Thrace, and Memnon, who entered the field
with 20,000 Affyrians and Ethiopians.   Many
of the adjacent cities were reduced and plundered, before the Greeks approached the walls
of Troy.   This City was the capital of Troas,
or according to fome, a country of which Ilium
was the Capital.   It was built on a fmall emi-
nence, near Mount Ida, and the Promontory
of Sigæum, at the diftance of about four miles
from the fea fhore.   Dardanus, the firft king of
the country, called it after him Dardania, from
Tros, one of his fucceffors, it was called Troja,
and from Ilus, Ilion.   Of all the the wars car-
carried on among the Ancients, that of Troy
is the moft famous.   When the fiege was begun, the enemies on both fides gave proofs of
valour and intrepidity.   The army of the
Greeks, however, was vifited by a plague, and
the operations were not lefs retarded by the
quarrel of Agamemnon and Achilles, celebrated
in the Iliad of Homer.   The lofs was great on
both fides, and the moft valiant of the Trojans,
particularly of the fons of Priam, were flain in
the field ; among thefe fell the Great Hector by
the hand of Achilles, and Paris, after having
flain

flain Achilles, was himfelf mortally wounded by one of the arrows of Philoctetes, which had once belonged to Hercules. After the fiege had been carried on for ten years, fome of the Trojans betrayed the city into the hands of the enemy, and Troy was reduced to afhes. The Poets, however, maintain that the Greeks made themfelves mafters of the place by artifice. . They fecretly filled a large wooden horfe with armed men, and led away their army from the plains, as if to return home. The Trojans brought this fatal horfe into their city, and in the night the Greeks that were inclofed within it, rufhed out, and opened the gates to their companions, who had returned from the place of their concealment. The greateft part of the inhabitants were put to the fword; among whom was the unhappy old King, who was favagely flaughtered by Pyrrhus, the fon of Achilles, and the queen with her daughters, and many others, were carried away Captives by the victors. This happened about 1270 years before the Chriftian Era, in the 3444th year of the Julian period. When Paris was killed, in the ninth year of the war, Helen married his brother Deiphobus, and when Troy was taken, fhe is faid to have betrayed him to the Greeks, in order to ingratiate herfelf with Menelaus,

E   whofe

whose forgiveness she obtained, and returned
with him to Sparta. But there is a tradition,
which says, that Paris was driven, as he returned from Sparta, upon the coast of Egypt,
where Proteus, king of the country, refused to
receive him, on account of his treachery to
Menelaus; he however detained Helen, and
Menelaus, by visiting Egypt as he returned
home, recovered her at the Court of Proteus,
and was too late convinced that the Trojan war
had been undertaken upon very unjust grounds.
This war proved little less deplorable in its conse-
quences to the victors than to the vanquished;
besides the great numbers that were slain before
the walls of Troy, many of those who departed
triumphant, perished on their return; far the
greatest part never more beheld their native
land, and several of the Chiefs who did at
length arrive in their dominions, instead of
enjoying the glory and the repose which they
expected would crown their long and painful
labours, found at home new wars and new
dangers to encounter, from the treachery and
ambition of those who had abused the authority
with which these princes had entrusted them
during their absence.   Agamemnon himself
was basely murdered at his return to his kingdom by Egisthus, who had usurped his throne
and bed, and by Clytemnestra his wife, the sister

of

of Helen. Ulyffes, King of Ithaca, whofe wifdom and fufferings are celebrated in the Odeffey
of Homer, after having been toffed by contrary winds, and fhipwrecked many times
during the fpace of ten years after the deftruction of Troy, through all which dangers he was
protected by the Goddefs Minerva, was at laft,
by her aid, happily re-eftablifhed in the poffeffion of his kingdom, and of his wife Penelope,
the moft virtuous and prudent of her fex.

To return to the Goddefs Venus, to whom
all thefe calamities have been attributed ; her
worfhip was univerfally eftablifhed, temples
and ftatues were erected to her in every kingdom, and the Ancients were fond of paying
homage to a divinity, by whofe influence mankind exifted. In her facrifices, and in the feftivals celebrated in her honor, too much licentioufnefs prevailed. Victims were feldom offered to her, or her altars ftained with blood.
No pigs, or male animals were deemed accepta-
ble. The rofe, the myrtle, and the apple were
facred to Venus ; among birds, the dove, the
fwan, and the fparrow were her favourites, and
among fifhes thofe called the Aphya, and the
Lycoftomus. The Goddefs of Beauty was reprefented among the Ancients in different forms.

E 2   At

At Elis she appeared seated on a goat, with one foot resting on a tortoise. At Sparta and Cythera, she was represented armed like Minerva, and sometimes wearing chains on her feet. In the temple of Jupiter Olympius, she was represented by Phidas, as rising from the sea, received by Love, and crowned by the Goddess of Persuasion. At Cnidus, her statue made by Praxiteles, was naked; that at Eliphantis was the same, with a naked Cupid by her side. In Sicyon, she held a poppy in one hand, and in the other an apple; while on her head she wore a crown, which terminated in a point, to intimate the pole. She is frequently represented with her son Cupid, on a chariot drawn by doves, or by swans, and sometimes by sparrows.

The firnames of this Goddess are numerous, and they serve to shew how well established her worship was all over the earth. She was called Cypria, because particularly adored in the island of Cyprus. She received the name of Paphia, on account of the worship paid her at Paphos, where she had a temple, with an altar, on which rain never fell, though it was exposed in the open air. Some of the ancients called her Apostrophia, or Epistrophia, as also Venus Urania, and Venus Pandemos. The first of
these

thefe names fhe received as prefiding over fenfual enjoyments ; the fecond, becaufe fhe likewife patronifed virtuous love, and chafte and mo-
derate gratifications; and the third, becaufe fhe
favoured the propenfities of the vulgar and im-
modeft. The Cnidians raifed her temples under the name of Aeræa of Doris, and of Euplœa.
In her temple under the name of Euplœa at Cnidus, was the moft celebrated of her ftatues : it
was made of white marble, and was one of the
moft perfect pieces of Praxiteles. Venus was
alfo firnamed Cytherea, becaufe fhe was the
chief deity of Cythera ; Expolis, becaufe her ftatue was without the city at Athens ; Philom-
meis, becaufe the Queen of Laughter. Tele-
pigama, becaufe fhe prefided over Mairiage ;
Coliada, Colotis, or Colias, becaufe worfhipped on a promontory of the fame name in Attica; Area, becaufe fometimes armed like Mars ;
Verticordia, becaufe fhe could turn the hearts of
women to chaftity ; Apaturia, becaufe fhe
deceived; Erycina, becaufe worfhipped at Eryx ;
Etaira, becaufe the patronefs of Courtezans;
Acidalia, becaufe of a fountain of Orchomenos.
Bafilea, becaufe the queen of Love ; Myrtea,
becaufe the myrtle was facred to her ; Liber-
tina, from her inclination to illicit pleafures ;
Mechanitis, in allufion to the many artifices
practifed in love, &c. &c. As Goddefs of the

Sea,

Sea, being born in the bofom of the waters, Venus was called Pontia, Marina, Limnefia, Epipontia, Pelagia, Saligenia, Pontogenia, Aligena, Thalaffia, &c. ; and as rifing from the fea, the name of Anadyomene is applied to her, and rendered immortal by the celebrated painting of Appelles, which reprefented her as iffuing from the bofom of the waves, and wringing her treffes on her fhoulders.

THE GRACES,

ATTENDANTS ON VENUS.

THE Graces, called alfo Charites, were faid to be the daughters of Venus, by Jupiter, or Bacchus. They were three in number, Algaia, Thalia, and Euphrofyne. They were the conftant attendants on the Goddefs of Beauty, and were reprefented as three young, beautiful, and modeft virgins, all holding each other by the hand. They prefided over kindnefs, and all good offices, and their worfhip was the fame as that of the nine Mufes, with whom they had a temple in common. They
were

were generally reprefented naked, becaufe kindneffes ought to be done with fincerity and candour. The moderns explain the allegory of their holding their hands joined, by obferving that there ought to be a perpetual and never ceafing intercourfe of kindnefs and benevolence among friends. Their youth denotes that the kindneffes which we have received ought ever to be frefh in our remembrance, and their virgin purity and innocence teach us, that acts of benevolence fhould be done without any expectation of reward, and that the favours we confer fhould be free from all interefted motives.

LATONA.

LATONA.

LATONA, the daughter of Cœus, the Titan, was a favourite miſtreſs of Jupiter, and the mother of Apollo and Diana, to whom ſhe gave birth in the iſland of Delos, which Neptune pitying her diſtreſs, and the perſecutions which ſhe ſuffered from the jealous rage of Juno, raiſed out of the ſea for her reception; but the repoſe ſhe enjoyed there was of ſhort duration, for Juno ſoon diſcovered the place of her retreat, and obliged her to fly from Delos. She wandered over the greateſt part of the world; and, in Caria, finding herſelf obliged to ſtop, being overcome with fatigue and heat, and almoſt fainting for thirſt, having diſcovered a ſpring in the bottom of a valley, ſhe run eagerly to it, and fell on her knees to drink of the refreſhing ſtream, but ſome peaſants, who chanced to be there, prevented her, and, in a ſurly manner, bid her depart. She earneſtly begged leave to drink; ſhe did not aſk, ſhe ſaid, to diſturb the water by waſhing herſelf in it, but only to quench her thirſt, which was intolerable. They

paid

paid no regard to her entreaties, but with many threats endeavoured to drive her away, and left they fhould drink, they leaped into the water, and muddied the ftream. This inhuman infolence provoked the indignation of Latona; fhe entreated Jupiter to punifh their barbarity, and they were immediately changed into frogs. The vengeance which Latona took on the proud and infolent Niobe has been already related, and the affiftance of Apollo and Diana was ever ready at the command of their mother. They deftroyed likewife with their arrows the Giant Tityus, who had attempted to offer her violence. At length Latona, though perfecuted and expofed to the refentment of Juno, became a powerful Deity. She faw her children receive divine honours, and her own worfhip was generally eftablifhed in thofe places where adoration was paid to them; particularly at Argos, Delos, &c. where fhe had temples. She had likewife an Oracle in Egypt, celebrated for the true and decifive anfwers which it gave.

E 5 DIANA.

DIANA.

THOUGH Diana is generally called the Goddefs of the Woods, and of Hunting, and may therefore be confidered as a terreſtrial Deity; yet, as ſhe was ſuppofed to be the fame as the Moon, and as her power and dignity were great, ſhe may juſtly be ranked among the celeſtial Divinities. A threefold character has indeed been aſcribed to this Goddeſs; in Heaven ſhe was Cynthia, or the Moon; on Earth Diana, the Huntreſs; and, in the infernal regions, Hecate, which is thought to be the fame as Proferpine, and, from that circumſtance, ſhe was called Triformis. According to Cicero, there were three Diana's, a daughter of Jupiter and Proferpine, who became the mother of Cupid; a daughter of Jupiter and Latona; and a daughter of Upis and Glauca; the fecond is the moſt celebrated, and to her all the ancients alluded. She had ſuch an averſion to marriage, that ſhe demanded of her father the permiſſion to live in perpetual celibacy, which was granted her. To ſhun the ſociety of the male ſex, ſhe devoted

herſelf

herfelf to hunting, and was always attended by a number of chofen virgins, who had, like her-felf, abjured marriage. Diana has, by fome, been fuppofed the fame as the Ifis of the Egyptians, whofe worfhip was introduced into Greece with that of Ofiris, under the name of Apollo. When Typhon waged war againft the Gods, Diana metamorphofed herfelf into a cat to avoid his fury, whence the particular vene-ration of the Egyptians for that animal. Al-pheus, a River God, falling in love with the nymph Arethufa, and purfuing her, Diana changed the nymph into a fountain, which bears her name; this fountain is in Ortygia, a fmall ifland near Syracufe, and the ancients affirm, that the river Alpheus, paffing under the fea from Peloponnefus, and without mingling itfelf with the falt waters, rifes again at Ortygia, and joins the ftream of Arethufa. If any thing is thrown into the Alpheus, in Elis, according to their traditions, it will re-appear after fome time fwimming in the waters of Areth , near Sicily. Meleager, fon of Œneus in Etolia, by Althea, daughter of Theftius, s punifhed by Diana for the fault of his fat , who had neglected the altars of the Gods . The Parcæ were prefent at birth of this hero, and predicted his future greatnefs, C. and

and Lachefis both foretold his uncommon strength and valour, and Atropos faid, he fhould live as long as a log of wood, which was then on the fire, remained unconfumed. Althea no fooner heard this, than fhe fnatched the brand from the fire, and kept it with the moft jealous care, as the life of her fon depended upon its prefervation. The fame of Maleager encreafed with his years ; he fignalized himfelf in the Argonautic expedition, and afterwards delivered his country from the neighbouring inhabitants, who made war againft his father at the inftigation of Diana. No fooner were they vanquifhed, than the vindictive Deity punifhed the negligence of Œneus, by a greater calamity. She fent a huge wild boar, which laid wafte all the country, and feemed invincible on account of its immenfe fize. It foon became a public concern, all the neighbouring Princes affembled to deftroy this terrible animal, and nothing is more famous in mythological hiftory, than the chace of the Calydonian boar. Among the princes and heroes who affembled on this occafion, were Meleager, Dryas, a fon of Mars; Caftor, and Pollux, fons of Jupiter and Leda; Thefeus, and his friend Perithous; Jafon, the leader of the Argonauts; Peleus and Telamon; Jolas, the friend of Hercules; Neftor,

afterwards

afterwards fo famed for his age and wifdom;
Laertes, the father of Ulyffes; Toxeus and
Plexippus, the brothers of Althea; and Atalanta,
the daughter of Schœneus. This armed troop
attacked the boar with uncommon fury, and it
was at laft killed by Meleager. The conqueror
gave the fkin and the head to Atalanta, who
had firft wounded the animal. This partiality
to a woman, irritated the others, and particularly the brothers of Althea. As they were
endeavouring to rob Atalanta of the honourable
prefent, Meleager defended a woman of whom
he was enamoured, and killed both his uncles
in the conteft. Mean time the news of this
celebrated conqueft had reached Calydon, and
Althea haftened to the temple of the Gods, to
return thanks for the victory which her fon had
obtained: As fhe went fhe met the corpfes of
her brothers, which were brought from the
chace, and at this mournful fpectacle fhe filled
the whole city with her cries and lamentations;
but when informed that they had been killed by
Meleager, in the firft tranfports of her grief
and rage, fhe refolved to revenge their death,
and flying to the place where fhe had laid up the
fatal brand, on which her fon's life depended,
fhe feized, and threw it into the fire, and Meleager died as foon as it was confumed. Homer
does

does not mention the fire-brand, whence some
have imagined that this fable is posterior to that
poet's age.   Actæon, a famous hunter, son of
Aristæus, was severely punished by Diana, for
having dared to look at her when she was
bathing in a fountain.   The Goddess, exaspe-
rated at his boldness, threw some of the water
in his face, when he was instantly transformed
into a stag, and was afterwards devoured by
his own dogs.

Though Diana was the patroness of Chastity,
yet she forgot her profession and her dignity, to
enjoy the company of the shepherd Endymion,
with whose beauty she was struck as she saw
him sleeping on mount Latmos.   The fable of
Endymion's amours with Diana has been
thought to arise from his knowledge of astro-
nomy ; and, as he passed the night on some high
mountain to observe the heavenly bodies, it
has been said that he was courted by the Moon.
Some authors have likewise asserted, that the
God Pan, notwithstanding his deformity, had
the good fortune to please this Goddess ; and it
has even been said that Orion was beloved of
her ; but that Aurora, who also loved him,
having carried him away into the island of Delos,
that she might enjoy his company with greater
                                        security,

fecurity, Diana being enraged with jealoufy, killed Orion with her arrows; but fome relate on the contrary, that the refentment of Diana againſt Orion, was occafioned by his having offered violence to Opis, one of her nymphs, and, according to others, it was becaufe he had attempted the virtue of the Goddefs herfelf.

Diana is reprefented with a bow in her hand, and a quiver full of arrows hanging from her fhoulder; and fhe is fometimes drawn in a chariot by two white ſtags. Sometimes fhe appears with wings, holding a lion in one hand, and a panther in the other, with a chariot drawn by two heifers, or two horfes of different co-lours. She is reprefented tall and robuſt, but beautiful and well fhaped. Her legs are bare, and her feet covered with a bufkin, worn by huntreffes among the ancients, and fhe is ge-generally diſtinguifhed in the figures that repre-fent her, by the crefcent on her head, by her hunting habit, and by the dogs which attend her. The moſt famous of her temples was at Ephefus, and it was one of the Seven Wonders of the World; fhe was there reprefented with many fymbols, which fignified the Earth or Cybele. Some of her ſtatues reprefented her with three heads, that of a horfe, a dog, and a boar.

boar. This Goddess received many sirnames from the places where her worship was established, and from the functions over which she presided. She was called Lucina Ilythia, or Juno Pronuba, when invoked by women in child-bed; and Trivia, when worshipped in the cross-ways, where her statues were generally erected. She was also called Agrotera, Orthia, Taurica, D ia, Aricia, &c. The inhabitants of Taurica were particularly attached to the worship of Diana, and they cruelly offered on her altar all the strangers that were shipwrecked on their coasts. Her temple in Aricia was served by a priest, who had always murdered his predecessor, and the Lacedemonians yearly offered her human victims; till the age of Lycurgas, who changed this barbarous custom for the sacrifice of flagellation. The Athenians generally offered her goats, and others a white kid, and sometimes a boar-pig, or an ox. Among plants, the poppy and the dittany were sacred to her. She, as well as her brother Apollo, had Oracles, among which those of Egypt, Cicilia, and Ephesus, are the most known.

When the Greeks, going to the Trojan war, were detained by contrary winds at Aulis, they

were

were informed by one of the foothfayers, that,
to appeafe the Gods, they muft facrifice Iphigenia, the daughter of Agamemnon, to Diana.
The father, who had provoked the Goddefs,
by killing her favourite ftag, heard this with
the greateft horror and indignation, and rather
than fhed the blood of his daughter, he commanded a herald (as chief of the Grecian forces)
to order all the affembled troops to depart to
their refpective homes; but Ulyffes, and the
other Generals, having interfered, Agamemnon
at laft confented to immolate his daughter for
the common caufe of Greece. As Iphigenia
was tenderly loved by her mother, the Greeks
fent for her, under pretext of giving her in
marriage to Achilles. Clytemneftra thus deceived, permitted her departure, and Iphigenia
came to Aulis; there fhe beheld the bloody
preparations for the facrafice, and found that
fhe herfelf was the deftined victim. She implored in vain the protection of her father;
Chalcas already held the knife, but juft as he
was about to ftrike the fatal blow, Iphigenia
fuddenly difappeared, and a goat of uncommon fize and beauty was found in her place for
the facrifice. This fupernatural change animated the Greeks, and the wind becoming favourable, the combined fleet fet fail from Aulis.
The

The youth and innocence of Iphigenia had raifed the compaffion of the Goddefs on whofe altar fhe was going to be facrificed. She conveyed her to Taurica, where fhe entrufted her with the care of her temple. In this facred office, Iphigenia was obliged, by the command of Diana, to facrifice all the ftrangers which came into that country. Many victims had already ftained the bloody altar ; when Oreftes, the brother of Iphigenia, and his friend Pylades, came to Taurica. Oreftes had avenged the death of his father, by that of his mother and Egifthus, and being afterwards perfecuted by the Furies for this deed, he confulted the Oracle of Apollo at Delphi, where he was informed that nothing could reftore him to peace, unlefs he could bring into Greece the ftatue of Diana, which was in the Taurica Cherfonefus. The enterprife was arduous, for it was well known that all ftrangers were facrificed on their arrival in that country. Oreftes and his friend were immediately carried before Thoas, the king of the place, and they were doomed to bleed on the altar of the Goddefs ; but Iphigenia finding they were Greeks, was touched with their misfortune, and offered to fpare the life of one of them, provided he would convey letters to Greece from her hand. The conteft
which

which enfued between Pylades and Oreftes, in
which each infifted on being immolated in order
to preferve his friend, has rendered their friendfhip proverbial, and their names immortal.   At
laft Pylades yielded with much reluctance ; but
when the Prieftefs delivered her letters to his
cure, he found they were addreffed to Oreftes,
and Iphigenia was informed that the man fhe
was about to immolate was her brother.   She
was no fooner convinced of it, than fhe fled
with the two friends from Cherfonefus, and
they carried away the ftatue of Diana.   Their
flight being difcovered Thoas prepared to purfue them, but Minerva interfered, and told him
that all had been done by the approbation and
will of the Gods. After thefe adventures, Oreftes
afcended the throne of Argos, and married
Hermione, the daughter of Menelaus and Helen.

AURORA.

AURORA.

AURORA, Goddefs of the Morning, daughter of Hyperion and Thia or Thea. Some fay that Pallas, fon of Crius, and brother to Perfes, was her father, hence the firname of Pallantias. She married Aftræus, by whom fhe had the Winds, the Stars, &c. Her amours with Tithonus and Cephalus, are alfo famous; fhe carried them both to Heaven, but Cephalus, who had married Procris, the daughter of Erechtheus, king of Athens, remained faithful to his wife, and was impatient to return, wherefore Aurora fent him back to her. Cephalus had been prefented by Procris with an unerring dart, which fhe had received from Diana; and, as he was fond of hunting, he every morning repaired to the woods, and paffed fo much time there, that Procris, alarmed by jealous fears, one day followed him thither fecretly. Cephalus, after much toil and fatigue, laid himfelf down in the cool fhade, and earneftly called for Aura, or the refrefhing breeze; this ambiguous word was miftaken for the name of a

miftrefs

miftrefs by the felf-deluded Procris, and fhe
eagerly raifed her head to fee what fhe believed
to be a rival; this movement occafioned a
ruftling among the leaves of the bufh that concealed her. Cephalus liftened, and thinking it
was fome wild beaft, he let fly his unerring
dart, and it ftruck Procris to the heart, who
expired in the arms of her hufband, confeffing
the ill-grounded jealoufy which was the caufe
of her death. Tithonus was the fon of Laomedon, king of Troy, by Strymo, the daughter of the Scamander ; he was fo beautiful, that
Aurora became enamoured of him, and carried him away; he had by her Memnon. The
Goddefs, at the requeft of Tithonus, obtained
of the Fates immortality for him; but as fhe
had forgotten to afk them to grant him likewife
a continuance of health, youth, and beauty, he
became at laft fo old, infirm, and decrepid, that
life became a burthen to him, and he prayed
Aurora to remove him from the world ; but as
that was no longer in her power, fhe changed
him into a grafshopper, which is faid to moult
when it is old, and grow young again. Memnon, their fon, went to the fiege of Troy to
affift king Priam ; he was flain by Achilles,
and in the place where he fell a fountain arofe,
which every year, on the fame day on which
                                          he

he died, flowed in blood inftead of water ; and,
as his body lay on the funeral pile to be burned,
it was changed into a bird by his mother
Aurora, and many other birds of the fame kind
flew out of the pile with him ; thefe dividing
themfelves into two troops, and furioufly fight-
ing with their beaks and claws, appeafed, with
their own blood, the ghoft of Memnon from
whom they fprung.   There was a ftatue of
Memnon made of black marble, in the temple of
Serapis, at Thebes in Egypt, of which an incredible ftory is related, for it is faid, that the
mouth of this ftatue, when firft touched by rays of
the rifing fun, fent forth a fweet and harmonious
found, as if it rejoiced at the appearance of
Aurora ; but, at the clofe of the day, it fent
forth a low and melancholy tone, as if it
lamented her departure.   Aurora had likewife
an intrigue with Orion, whom fhe carried
to the ifland of Delos, where he was killed by
Diana's arrows.

This Goddefs is ufualy reprefented by the
poets as drawn in a rofe coloured chariot, and
opening with her rofy fingers the gates of the
Eaft, pouring the dew upon the earth, and
making the flowers grow.   Her chariot is generally

nerally drawn by white horfes, and fhe is covered with a veil. Nox and Somnus fly before her, and the conftellations of Heaven difappear at her approach. She always fets out before the Sun, and is the forerunner of his rifing. The Greeks call her Eos.

TERRESTRIAL GODS.

| SATURN | VULCAN |
| JANUS | MOMUS |

ÆOLUS, AND THE WINDS.

SATURN.

SATURN was a fon of Cœlus, or Uranus, by Terra, called alfo Titea, Thea, or Titheia; he was naturally artful, and, with the affiftance of his mother, he revenged himfelf on his father, whofe cruelty to his children had provoked the anger of Thea. Cœlus was mutilated, and difpoffeffed of his kingdom, and his fons, whom he had confined in the infernal regions, were reftored to liberty. Saturn obtained the kingdom by the confent of his brother Titan, on condition that he fhould not bring up any male children. Purfuant to this agreement, Saturn always devoured his fons as foon as born, and becaufe, as fome obferve, he dreaded from them a retaliation of the illtreatment he had fhewn his father; but his wife Rhea, unwilling to fee all her fons perifh, when Jupiter was born concealed him, and wrapped up a large ftone which fhe gave her hufband inftead of the child, and which he immediately fwallowed without perceiving the deception. She likewife preferved Neptune and Pluto in the fame manner. Titan was fome time after informed that Saturn had concealed his male
children,

children, whereupon he made war againft him, and having dethróned, kept him in confinement with Rhea. Jupiter, who was fecretly educated in Crete, was no fooner grown up than he flew to deliver them, and replaced his father on his throne. But Saturn, unmindful of his fon's kindnefs, became jealous of his glory, and con- fpired to ruin him ; and Jupiter having dif- covered *this*, depofed and banifhed him from Heaven. The father fled for fafety into Italy, which country had the name of La- tium, from being the place of his conceal- ment. Janus, who was then king of Italy, received Saturn with great hofpitality and kind- nefs ; he even made him his partner on the throne, ·and the king of Heaven employed him- felf in civilizing the barbarous manners of the people of Italy, and in teaching them agricul- ture, and the ufeful and liberal arts. His reign there was fo mild and popular, fo beneficent and virtuous, that thofe times have been called the *Golden Age*, to intimate the happinefs and tranquillity which the earth then enjoyed. The Silver Age fucceeded, in which mankind began to degenerate, and their peaceful ftate was dif- turbed by the feuds and diffentions which arofe amongft them. Next came the Brazen Age, in which licentioufnefs and avarice took poffeffion of the human heart, and laftly, the Iron Age,

when

when the world being funk into univerfal depravity, war and bloodfhed made up the mea-
fure of the crimes and miferies of its inhabitants. Thefe are the four ages of the world,
mentioned by the poets, and followed by the
Deluge, which is said to have happened in the
reign of Deucalion, a king of Theffaly. The
impiety of mankind had irritated Jupiter, who
refolved to deftroy the whole race of men, and
immediately the earth exhibited a boundlefs
fcene of waters. The higheft mountains were
climbed by the affrighted inhabitants of the
country; but thefe feeming places of fecurity
were foon overflowed by the rifing waters, and
left no hope of efcaping the univerfal calamity.
Deucalion was a fon of Prometheus, and had
married Pyrrha, the daughter of Epimetheus.
Jupiter fpared this virtuous pair, and Deucalion
was directed to embark with his wife Pyrrha
in a fhip, which he accordingly did. The
veffel was toffed about during nine fucceffive
days; at the end of which it refted on the
top of mount Parnaffus, where Deucalion remained till the waters had fubfided. As foon
as they had retired from the furface of the earth,
Deucalion and his wife went to confult the
Oracle of Themis, and were directed to reftore
the human race, by throwing behind them the

bones

bones of their great Mother. After fome he-
fitation about the meaning of the Oracle, they
obeyed, by cafting behind them ftones, which
they underftood to be the bones of their Mother,
the Earth. The ftones thrown by Deucalion
became men, and thofe of Pyrrha women.
According to fome writers, this Deluge did not
overflow the whole earth, but only the country
of Theffaly; and they fay it was produced by
the inundation of the waters of the river Peneus,
whofe regular courfe was ftopped by an earthquake near mount Offa and Olympus. According to Xenophon, there were no lefs than
five Deluges. That of Deucalion, fo much
celebrated, happened about 1380, or 90 years
before the Chriftian æra.

The worfhip of Saturn was not fo folemn, or
fo univerfal as that of Jupiter. It was ufual
to offer human victims on his altars; but this
barbarous cuftom was abolifhed by Hercules,
who fubftituted fmall images of clay. In the
facrifices of Saturn, the prieft always performed
the ceremonies with his head uncovered, which
was ufual at other folemnities. The God is
generally reprefented as an old man, bowed
with infirmities; he holds a fcythe in his right
hand, with a ferpent, which bites its its own

tail, and which is an emblem of time, and of the revolution of the year. In his left hand he holds a child raifed up, as if about to devour it. Tatius, king of the Sabines, firft built a temple to Saturn on the Capitoline hill, a fecond was afterwards erected by Tullus Hoftilius, and a third by the firft Confuls. On his ftatues were ufually hung fetters, in commemoration of the chains he had worn when imprifoned by Jupiter. From this circumftance all flaves, that obtained their liberty, generally dedicated their fetters to him. During the celebration of the Saturnalia, the chains were taken from the ftatues, to intimate the freedom and independance which mankind had enjoyed during the Golden Age. One of the temples of this God at Rome, was appropriated for the public treafury, and it was there alfo that the names of foreign ambaffadors were enrolled.

Saturn was fuppofed to be the father of the Centaur Chiron, by Philyra, whom he changed into a mare, to deceive the fufpicions of his wife Rhea.

JANUS.

JANUS.

JANUS was the moſt ancient king who reigned in Italy. He was a native of Theſſaly, and, according to ſome, ſon of Apollo ; other authors make him ſon of Cœlus and Hecate ; and others make him a native of Athens. He came to Italy, where he planted a colony, and built a ſmall town on the river Tiber, which he called Janiculum. During his reign, Saturn, as has been related, driven from Heaven by his ſon Jupiter, came to Italy, where Janus received him with hoſpitality, and made him his colleague on the throne. After death, Janus was ranked among the Gods for his popularity, and the civilization which he, in concert with Saturn, had introduced among the wild inhabitants of Italy. Janus is repreſented with two faces, becauſe he was ſuppoſed to be acquainted with the paſt and future ; or, according to ſome, becauſe he was taken for the Sun, who opens the day at his riſing, and ſhuts it at his ſetting. Some ſtatues repreſent this Deity with four heads. He was ſometimes ſeen with

a beard,

a beard, and fometimes without. In religious ceremonies, his name was always invoked the firft, becaufe he prefided over all gates and avenues; and it was through him only, that prayers were believed to reach the Celeftial Gods; from that idea, he often appears with a key in his right hand, and a rod in his left. Sometimes he holds the number 300 in cne hand, and in the other 65, to fhew that he prefides over the year, of which the firft month bears his name. Some fuppofe that he is the fame as the World, or Cœlus; and, from that fuppofition, they call him Eanus, becaufe of the revolution of the heavens. He was called Quirinius, or Martialis, becaufe he prefided over war; he was alfo called Patulcius, and Claufius, becaufe the gates of his temples were opened during the time of war, and kept fhut in time of peace; and it appears that they were fhut by the Romans only three times during more than 700 years; once by Numa; the fecond time by the confuls Marcus Attilius, and Titus Manlius, after the Carthaginian war; and, laftly, by Auguftus, after the victory of Actium. This God was chiefly worfhipped at Rome, where he had many temples; fome erected to Janus Bifrons, others to Janus Quadrifons. The temples of Quadrifons were built with four

equal

equal fides, with a door, and three windows on
each fide ; the four doors were the emblems of
the four Seafons of the year, and the three windows in each of the fides, that of the three
months of each feafon, and all together of the
twelve months of the year.   Janus was generally reprefented in ftatues as a young man.

VULCAN.

VULCAN was, according to Hefiod, the fon of Juno alone; but Homer makes him the fon of Jupiter and Juno, and fays, that his mother was fo difgufted with the deformity of her fon, that fhe threw him into the fea as foon as born, where he remained nine years. According to the more received opinion, Vulcan was educated in Heaven; but was kicked down from thence by his father to the earth, when he attempted to deliver his mother, whom Jupiter had fufpended from Heaven by a golden chain; he was nine days in defcending, and he fell in the ifland of Lemnos, where, according to Lucian, the inhabitants feeing him in the air, caught him in their arms; he however broke his leg in the fall, and ever after remained lame of one foot. He fixed his refidence in Lemnos, where he built himfelf a palace, and raifed forges to work metals; as he prefided over fire, and was the patron of all artifts who worked iron, and all kinds of metals. The inhabitants of the ifland became fenfible of the advantages

tages to be derived from the refidence of Vulcan
among them, and were taught by him all thofe
ufeful arts which could civilize their rude manners, and render them ufeful to fociety. The
firft work of Vulcan was, according to fome,
a throne for his mother, which was of gold,
and made with fecret fprings, and he prefented
it to Juno, to avenge himfelf for her want of
affection towards him. The Goddefs was no
fooner feated on this throne, than fhe found
herfelf unable to move. The Gods attempted
to deliver her, by breaking the chains by which
fhe was held, but to no purpofe, and Vulcan
alone had the power to fet her at liberty.
Bacchus intoxicated, and then prevailed upon
him to come to Olympus, where he was reconciled to his parents. Vulcan has been celebrated by the ancient poets, for the ingenious
works, and automatical figures which he made,
and many fpeak of two golden ftatues, which not
only feemed animated, but which walked by his
fide, and even affifted him in working of metals. It is faid, that at the requeft of Jupiter, he
made the firft woman that ever appeared on
earth, well known under the name of Pandora.
Jupiter meant to punifh the impiety and' artifice of Prometheus (who had ftolen fire from
Heaven, to animate the man which he had

made),

made), by giving him a wife. When the woman had been made of clay by the artift, and had received life from Jupiter, all the other Gods vied in making her prefents. Venus gave her beauty, and the Graces the power of captivating; Apollo taught her to fing; Mercury inftructed her in eloquence, and Minerva gave her the moft rich and fplendid ornaments. From all thefe valuable gifts which fhe had received from the Gods, the woman was called Pandora; which implies, that fhe was endowed with every neceffary quality. Jupiter laftly gave her a beautiful box, which fhe was ordered to prefent to the man who married her, and Mercury was commiffioned to conduct her to Prometheus; but that artful mortal was aware of the danger, and he fent away Pandora without fuffering himfelf to be captivated with her charms. His brother, Epimetheus, was not poffeffed of the fame prudence and fagacity; he married Pandora, and when he opened the box which fhe had given him, there iffued from it a multitude of evils and diftempers, which difperfed themfelves all over the world, and which, from that fatal moment, have never ceafed to afflict the human race. Hope alone remained at the bottom of the box; and it is that only which has the wonderful power of fupporting
man.

man under his labours, and of alleviating all his
pains and forrows. The moft known of the
works of Vulcan, which were prefented to mortals, are, a collar given to Hermione, the wife
of Cadmus, and a fceptre which was in the
poffeffion of Agamemnon. The collar proved
fatal to all who wore it; but the fceptre, after
the death of Agamemnon, was carefully preferved at Cheronea, and regarded as a Divinity.

The amours of Vulcan are not numerous.
He demanded Minerva in marriage; but his
addreffes being rejected by that Goddefs, Jupiter gave him one of the Graces, and Venus
is univerfally acknowledged to have been the
wife of Vulcan. Some Mythologifts affirm that
Vulcan was father of Cupid, who was generally reputed the fon of Mars. He was likewife by fome faid to be the father of Servius
Tullius, the fixth king of Rome, by Ocrifia,
the wife of Corniculus. Cecrops, Cœculus,
Cacus, Perephetes, Cercyon, and others,
have alfo been reputed his children. Cicero
fpeaks of more than one Deity of the name of
Vulcan; one he calls fon of Cœlus, and
father of Apollo, by Minerva; the fecond he
mentions, is fon of the Nile, and called Phtas,
by the Egyptians; the third was fon of Jupiter
and

and Juno, and fixed his refidence in Lemnos ; and the fourth, who built his forges in the Lipari iflands, was fon of Menalius. The worfhip of Vulcan was well eftablifhed, particularly in Egypt, at Athens, and at Rome. It was ufual in the facrifices which were offered to him, to burn the whole victim, and not referve part of it, as in the immolations to the other Gods. A calf, and a boar-pig, were the principal victims offered to him. Vulcan was reprefented covered with fweat, blowing with his nervous arm the fires of his forges. Some reprefent him lame and deformed, holding a hammer raifed ready to ftrike, while, with the other hand, he turns with pincers a thunder-bolt on his anvil. He fometimes appears with a long beard, difhevelled hair, half-naked, and a fmall round cap on his head, holding a hammer and pincers in his hand. The Egyptians reprefented him under the figure of a monkey. Vulcan has received the names of Mulciber, Pamphanes, Clytotechnes, Pandamator, Cyllopodes, Chalaipoda, &c. all expreffive of his lamenefs, and of his profeffion.

THE

THE CYCLOPS.

———

THE Cyclops were the minifters and attendants of Vulcan; and with him they fabricated
not only the thunder-bolts of Jupiter, but alfo
arms for the Gods, and for the moft celebrated
heroes. They were fuppofed to be the fons of
Cœlus and Terra; their ftature was gigantic,
and they had but one eye in the middle of the
forehead. According to Hefiod, the Cyclops
were three in number, and called Arges,
Brontes, and Steropes; but according to other
Mythologifts, their number was greater, and,
in the age of Ulyffes, Polyphemus, the fon of
Neptune, was their king: they inhabited the
weftern parts of the ifland of Sicily, and were
fuppofed to have forges under mount Etna.
The moft folid walls and impregnable fortreffes,
were faid, by the ancients, to have been the
work of the Cyclops, to render them more
refpectable. The Cyclops were reckoned
among the Gods, and we find a temple dedicated to their fervice at Corinth, where facrifices were folemnly offered.

The

The poets fpeak of the Cyclops as man-eaters. Some writers are of opinion, that the tradition of their having only one eye, might originate from their wearing fmall bucklers of fteel, which covered their faces, and had a fmall aperture in the middle, which cor-refponded exactly with the eye.

MOMUS.

MOMUS.

MOMUS, the God of Pleafantry, was the fon of Nox, according to Hefiod. He was continually fatyrizing the Gods, and whatever they did was freely turned to ridicule by him. He blamed Vulcan, becaufe, in the human form which he had made of clay, he had not placed a window in the breaft, by which means, whatever was done or thought there, might eafily have been perceived. He cenfured the houfe which Minerva had made, becaufe the Goddefs had not made it moveable ; by means of which a bad neighbourhood might have been avoided. In the bull which Neptune had produced, he obferved, that his blows might have been furer, if his eyes had been placed nearer his horns. Venus herfelf was expofed to his fatire ; and when the fneering God could find no defect in the perfect form of that Goddefs, he obferved, as fhe retired, that the noife of her feet was too loud, and extremely improper in the Goddefs of Beauty and Gracefulnefs. Thefe illiberal reflections, and impertinent ralleries,

leries, were highly difpleafing to all the Gods, and were the caufe that Momus was at length driven from Heaven. This God is generally reprefented raifing a mafk from his face, and holding a fmall figure in his hand.

ÆOLUS, AND THE WINDS.

ÆOLUS, the God of Storms and Winds, was the fon of Hippotas ; he reigned over Æolia, and becaufe he was the inventor of fails, and a great Aftronomer, the Poets have afcribed to him the power of commanding the winds. Homer relates, that he gave Ulyffes all the Winds that could impede his return to Ithaca, confined in a bag ; but the companions of Ulyffes, prompted by curiofity, untied the bag, and fet the winds at liberty. There are two others of the name of Æolus, a King of Etruria, Father to Macareus and Canace, and a fon of Hellenus, often confounded with the God of the Winds ; this laft married Enaretta, by whom he had feven fons and five daughters.

BOREAS.

BOREAS is the name of the North Wind, blowing from the Hyperborean Mountains.
According

According to the Poets, he was the son of Aſtræus and Aurora; others make him son of the Strymon. He was King of Thrace, and carried away by force Orithyia, a daughter of Erechtheus, King of Athens; he had by her Zetes and Calais, Cleopatra and Chione. He was worſhipped as a Deity, and the Athenians dedicated altars to him and the other Winds, when Xerxes invaded Europe. His ſons Zetes and Calais, accompanied the Argonauts to Colchis. Boreas is repreſented with wings and white hair; he appears always rough and ſhivering; and as the author of rain, ſnow, hail, and tempeſts, he is ſurrounded with impenetrable clouds.

ZEPHYRUS.

ZEPHYRUS, the Weſt Wind, ſon of Aſtræus and Aurora, the ſame as the Favonius of the Latins. He married a Nymph called Chloris, or Flora, by whom he had a ſon named Carpos. Zephyrus was ſaid to produce flowers and fruits by the ſweetneſs of his breath. He had a temple at Athens, where he was repreſented as a young man of a delicate form, with wings on his ſhoulders, and having his head covered with all ſorts of flowers.

EURUS.

EURUS.

EURUS, a Wind which blows from the East; the Latins sometimes call it Vulturnus. Eurus is reprefented as a young man flying with great impetuofity, and often appearing in a playful and wanton humour.

AUSTER.

AUSTER, a Wind which blows from the South, and generally produces diftempers. He is reprefented as an old man with grey hair, a gloomy countenance; his head covered with clouds, a fable vefture, and dufky wings. He is the difpenfer of heavy fhowers.

The Winds, according to fome Mythologifts, were confined by Æolus, in a large cave; and, without this neceffary precaution, they would have overturned the earth, and reduced every thing to its original chaos.

TERRESTRIAL GODDESSES.

VESTA   CERES

CYBELE   THEMUSES

THEMIS, ASTRÆA, NEMESIS.

VESTA.

VESTA, the daughter of Saturn and Rhea, and fifter to Juno and Ceres. She is often confounded by Mythologifts with Rhea, Ceres, Cybele, Proferpine, Hecate, and Tellus. When confidered as the mother of the Gods, fhe is the mother of Rhea and Saturn; and when confidered as the patronefs of the Veftal-Virgins, and the Goddefs of Fire, fhe is called the daughter of Saturn and Rhea; under this laft name fhe was worfhipped by the Romans. Æneas was the firft who introduced her Myf-teries into Italy, and Numa built her a temple, which no males were permitted to enter. The Palladium of Troy was fuppofed to be pre-ferved within her fanctuary, and a fire was continually kept burning by a certain number of Virgins, who had dedicated themfelves to the fervice of the Goddefs. If the fire of Vefta was ever extinguifhed, it was fuppofed to prog-nofticate fome fudden calamity to the Repub-lic. The Virgin, by whofe negligence it had been extinguifhed, was feverely punifhed, and

it

it was rekindled by the Rays of the Sun. The temple of Vefta was of a round form, and the Goddefs was reprefented in a long flowing robe, with a veil on her head ; holding in one hand a lamp, or a two eared veffel, and in the other a javelin, or fometimes a Palladium ; on fome medals fhe appears holding a drum in one hand, and a fmall figure of victory in the other.

The Goddefs is likewife called Terra, and under this name fhe is looked upon as one of the moft ancient Deities in Mythology; wife of Uranus or Cœlus, and mother of Saturn, Oceanus, the Titans, Giants, Cyclops, &c. She had many other names, but moft of them in common with Cybele, or the younger Vefta, of whom I fhall fpeak after having given fome account of the

VESTAL VIRGINS.

THEY were Priefteffes confecrated to the fervice of Vefta, as their name intimates. This office was very ancient, as the mother of Romulus was one of the Veftals. Æneas is fuppofed to have firft eftablifhed them. Numa appointed four, and Tarquin added two to that number. They were always chofen by the

G   monarchs,

monarchs, but after the expulsion of the Tarquins, the High Priest was entrusted with the
care of them : they were chosen young, from
the age of six, to ten; and if there was not a
sufficient number that presented themselves as
Candidates for the office, twenty Virgins were
selected, and those upon whom the lot fell, were
obliged to become Vestals. Plebeians as well
as patricians were allowed to propose themselves, though they were in general nobly born,
and it was required that they should be without blemish or deformity in every part of their
body. For thirty years they were to remain
in the strictest continence ; the ten first years
were spent in learning the duties of the order,
the ten following were employed in discharging
them with fidelity and sanctity, and the ten last
in instructing such as had entered into the No-
viciate : when the thirty years were elapsed,
they were permited to marry ; or, if they still
preferred celibacy, they waited upon the rest of
the Vestals. As soon as a Vestal was initiated,
her head was shaved, to intimate the liberty of
her person, as she was then free from the
shackles of parental authority, and she was permitted to dispose of her possessions as she thought
proper. The employment of the Vestals was,
as has been observed, to take care that the sacred

cred fire of Vefta was not extinguifhed ; and if
it ever happened to be fo, the offender was for her,
negligence feverely fcourged by the High Prieft..
In fuch a cafe all was confternation at Rome,
as it was deemed the prognoftic of great calamities to the ftate, and the fire was again kindled
by glaffes, with the rays of the fun. -Another
equally particular charge of the Veftals, was to
guard a facred pledge, on which was thought
to depend the very exiftence of Rome.   This,
according to fome, was the Palladium of Troy,
others pretend it was fome of the Myfteries of
the Gods of Samothrace. The privileges of
the Veftals were great, they had the moft honourable feats at public games and feftivals.
A lictor, with the fafces, always preceded them
when they walked in public.   They were carried in chariots when they pleafed, and they had
the power of pardoning criminals when led to execution, if they declared that their meeting them
was accidental.   Their declarations in trials
were received without the formality of an oath.
They were chofen .as Arbitors in caufes of
moment, and in the execution of wills ; and fo
great was the deference paid them by the Ma-
giftrates, as well as by the people, that the confuls themfelves made way for them, and bowed
their faces when they paffed before them.   To

infult

infult them was a capital crime, and whoever attempted to violate their chaſtity, was beaten to death with ſcourges. If any of them died while in office, the body was buried within the walls of the city, an honour granted to few. Such of the Veſtals as proved incontinent, were puniſhed in the moſt rigorous manner. Numa ordered them to be ſtoned, but Tarquin the elder, cauſed a large hole to be dug in the earth, where a bed was placed, with a little bread, wine, water and oil, and a lighted lamp. The guilty Veſtal was then ſtriped of the habit of her order, and compelled to deſcend into the ſubterraneous cavity, which was immediately ſhut, and ſhe was left to periſh there. Few however of the Veſtals were found guilty of in-continence, and for the ſpace of one thouſand years, during which the order continued eſta-bliſhed, from the reign of Numa, only eighteen were puniſhed for the violation of their vow. The Veſtals were aboliſhed by Theodoſius the Great, and the fire of Veſta extinguiſhed. The dreſs of the Veſtals was peculiar, they wore a white veſt, with purple borders, a white linen ſurplice, above which a large purple mantle, which flowed to the ground, and which was tucked up when they offered ſacrifices. They had a cloſe covering on their head, from which
hung

hung ribbons. Their manner of living was fumptuous, as they were maintained at the public expence, and though originally fatisfied with the fimple diet of the Romans, their tables foon after difplayed the fuperfluities and luxuries of the great and opulent.

CYBELE.

C YBELE, a daughter of Cœlus and Terra, and wife of Saturn. She is sometimes called Rhea, Ops, Vesta, Bona Mater, Magna Mater, Bona Dea, Berecynthia, Dindymene, &c. According to Diodorus, she was the daughter of a Lydian Prince, and as soon as she was born was exposed on a mountain. She was preserved by sucking some of the wild beasts of the forest, and received the name of Cybele from the Mountain where her life had been preserved. When she returned to her father's court, she fell in love with a beautiful youth, whose name was Atys. All the Mythologists are unanimous in mentioning the amours of Atys and Cybele. The partiality of the Goddess for this youth, seems to arise from his having first introduced her worship in Phrygia. The festivals of Cybele were there observed with the greatest solemnity. Her priests were called Corybantes, Galli, &c. and in the celebration of her festivals they imitated the behaviour of madmen, filling the air with shrieks and howling, ings, mixed with the confufed noife of drums, tabrets, bucklers and fpears. This was in commemoration of the forrow of Cybele for the lofs of her favourite Atys ; who, according to Ovid, was changed by the Goddefs into a pinetree, as he was about to lay violent hands upon himfelf, for having violated a vow of chaftity, which fhe had obliged him to take, and ever after that tree was facred to the mother of the Gods. Atys received divine honours, and temples were raifed to his memory, particularly at Dymæ.

Cybele was generally reprefented as a robuft woman, far advanced in her pregnancy, to intimate the fecundity of the earth ; fhe held keys in her hand, and her head was crowned with rifing turrets, and fometimes with the leaves of the Oak. She fometimes appears riding in a chariot drawn by two tame lions. Atys follows, carrying a ball in his hand, and fupporting himfelf upon a fir-tree, which is facred to the Goddefs. Sometimes fhe is reprefented with a fceptre in her hand, and her head covered with a tower : fhe is alfo feen with many beafts about her, and carrying two lions under her arms. From Phrygia, the worfhip of Cybele paffed into Greece, and was folemnly eftablifhed

G 4   at

at Eleufis, under the name of the Eleufinian
Myfteries of Ceres.   The Romans, by order
of the Sibyline books, brought the Statue of
this [Goddefs from Peffinus in Italy, and when
the fhip which carried it had run on a fhallow
bank of the Tiber, the virtue and innocence of
the Veftal Claudia (who had been accufed of
incontinence) was vindicated by her removing
it with her girdle.   It is fuppofed that the
Myfteries of Cybele were firft known about 257
years before the Trojan war, or 1580 years before the Auguftan age.   The Romans were
particularly fuperftitious in wafhing every year,
the fixth of the calends of April, the fhrine of
this Goddefs in the waters of the river Almon.
Too much indecency prevailed in the celebration of the feftivals, the example of which was
given by the Priefts themfelves.

CERES.

CERES, the Goddefs of Corn and of Harvefts, was the daughter of Saturn and Ops. She had a daughter by Jupiter, whom fhe called Proferpine. This daughter was carried away by Pluto, as fhe was gathering flowers in the plains near Enna. The lofs of Proferpine was grievous to Ceres, who fought her all over Sicily, and, when night came on, fhe lighted two torches in the flames of mount Ætna, in order to continue her fearch all over the world. She at laft found the veil of Proferpine near the fountain Cyane, but no intelligence could be obtained of the place of her concealment, till at length the nymph, Arethufa, informed the Goddefs, that her daughter had been carried away by Pluto. No fooner had Ceres received this information, than fhe flew to Heaven, and demanded of Jupiter the reftoration of her darling child. The God ufed his endeavour to reconcile her to Pluto as a fon-in-law; but his reprefentations proved fruitlefs, and the reftoration was granted, provided that Profer-

G 5   pine

pine had not eaten any thing in the kingdom
of Pluto. Ceres upon this repaired to the infernal regions, but Proferpine had eaten the
grains of a pomgranate, which she had gathered in the Elyfian-fields, and Afcalaphus having obferved her at that time, difcovered it to
Pluto. The return of Proferpine upon earth
was therefore impoffible, but Afcalaphus, for
his unfolicited information, was changed into
an owl. The grief of Ceres, for the lofs of
her daughter was fo violent, that Jupiter at
length decreed, Proferpine fhould pafs fix months
of the year with her mother, and the reft with
her hufband. During the enquiries of Ceres
for her daughter, the cultivation of the earth
had been neglected, and the ground became
barren ; therefore to repair the lofs which mankind had fuffered by her abfence, the Goddefs
went to Attica, which was become the moft
defolate country in the world, and inftructed
Triptolemus, the fon of Celeus, king of Attica,
in every thing which concerned agriculture.
Celeus had invited Ceres to his houfe, as fhe
travelled over the country in queft of her
daughter, and to repay his kindneffes the Goddefs took particular notice of his infant fon.
She nourifhed him with her own milk, and
placed him on burning coals during the night,

to

to deftroy whatever particles of mortality he had received from his parents. The mother was aftonifhed at the fudden growth of her fon, and had the curiofity to watch Ceres,. whom fhe difturbed by a fudden cry, when fhe beheld her child laid on the burning afhes ; and as that interruption rendered the Goddefs unable to make Triptolemus immortal, fhe taught him the manner of ploughing the earth, of fowing and reaping the corn, and of making bread, and by this means rendered him ferviceable and dear to mankind. She afterwards gave him her chariot, which was drawn by two dragons, and in this celeftial vehicle he travelled all over the world, diftributing corn to the inhabitants of it. In Scythia, the favourite of Ceres had nearly perifhed by the machinations of Lyncus, who reigned in that country, but this favage prince was punifhed for his intended crime, by being tranfformed into a Lynx. Triptolemus, at his return to Eleufis, eftablifhed there the feftivals in honour of Ceres ; he reigned for fome time, and after death received divine honours. Some fuppofe that he accompanied Bacchus in his Indian expedition. The beneficence of Ceres to mankind procured her great veneration. Sicily was fuppofed to be the favourite retreat of that Goddefs ; and Diodorus fays, that Ceres

G 6

and

Proferpine firſt appeared to mortals in that iſland, which Pluto received as a nuptial dowry from Jupiter when he married Proferpine. The Sicilians made a yearly ſacrifice to Ceres, every man according to his abilities; and the fountain Cyane, through which Pluto opened himfelf a paſſage with his trident, when carrying away Proferpine, was publicly honoured with an offering of bulls, and the blood of the victims was ſhed in the waters of the fountain. Befides theſe, other ceremonies were obſerved in honour of the two Goddeſſes, who had ſo peculiarly favoured the iſland. The commemoration of the Rape was celebrated about the beginning of the harveſt, and the ſearch of Ceres, at the time that corn is ſown into the earth. The latter feſtival continued ſix ſucfive days. Ceres performed alſo the duties of a legiſlator, and the Sicilians experienced great advantages from her ſalutary laws, hence her firname of Theſmophora. She is the fame as the Iſis of the Egyptians, and her worſhip was firſt brought into Greece by Erechtheus, about 1426 years before the Chriſtian æra, according to ſome authors. She met with various adventures in her travels over the earth, and the impudence of Stellio was feverely puniſhed, for he was changed into an elf by the Goddeſs, for

having

having derided her. A fow was offered in facrifice to Ceres, as that animal frequently injures and deftroys the productions of the earth. While the corn was yet in grafs, they offered her a ram, after the victim had been led three times round the field. Ceres was reprefented with a garland of ears of corn on her head, holding in one hand a lighted torch, and in the other a poppy, which was facred to her. She fometimes appears as a country woman, mounted upon the back of an ox, carrying a bafket on her left arm, and holding a hoe; and fometimes fhe rides in a chariot, drawn by winged dragons. She has been fuppofed by fome to be the fame as Rhea, Tellus, Cybele, Bona Dea, Berecynthia, &c. The Romans paid her great adoration, and her feftivals were celebrated annually by the Roman matrons, in the month of April, during eight days; thefe matrons abftained at that time from the ufe of wine, and any fenfual enjoyments; they always carried lighted torches, in commemoration of thofe carried by Ceres when in fearch of her daughter; and whoever came to thefe feftivals without a previous initiation, was punifhed with death. Ceres is metaphorically called bread and corn, as the word Bacchus is fometimes ufed to fignify wine.

THE

THE MUSES.

THE Muses were Goddesses, who presided over Poetry, Music, Dancing, and all the Liberal Arts. They were daughters of Jupiter and Mnemosyne, and were nine in number.

CLIO

PRESIDED over History. She is represented crowned with laurels, holding in one hand a trumpet, and a book in the other. Sometimes she holds a quill, with a lute. Her name signifies Honour and Reputation, and it was her office faithfully to record the actions of brave and illustrious heroes. She was mother of Hyacintha, by Pierus, son of Magnes.

UTERPE

PRESIDED over Music, and was looked upon as the inventress of the flute. She is represented

prefented as crowned with flowers, and holding a flute. Some Mythologifts have attributed to her the invention of Tragedy, more commonly fuppofed to be the production of Melpomene.

THALIA

PRESIDED over Feftivals, and over paftoral and comic Poetry. She is reprefented leaning on a column, holding a mafk in her right hand, by which fhe is diftinguifhed from her fifters, as alfo by a fhepherd's crook. Her drefs appears fhorter, and not fo much ornamented as that of the other Mufes.

MELPOMENE

PRESIDED over Tragedy. Horace has addrefled the fineft of his Odes to her, as to the patronefs of Lyric Poetry. She was generally reprefented with a ferious countenance and fplendid garments. She wore a bufkin, and held a dagger in one hand, and in the other a fceptre and crowns.

TERPSICHORE.

TERPSICHORE

PRESIDED over Dancing, of which fhe was reckoned the inventrefs, as her name intimates. She is reprefented like a young virgin, crowned with laurel, and holding in her hand a mufical inftrument.

ERATO

PRESIDED over lyric and tender Poetry. She is reprefented as crowned with rofes and myrtle, holding a lyre in her hand. She fometimes appears with a thoughtful, and fometimes with a gay and animated, look. She was invoked by lovers, efpecially in the month of April, which, among the Romans, was more particularly devoted to love.

POLYHYMNIA, or POLYMNIA,

PRESIDED over Singing and Rhetoric, and was deemed the inventrefs of Harmony. She

was

was reprefented veiled in white robes, holding
a fceptre in her left hand, and with her right
raifed up as ready to harangue. On her head
fhe wore a crown of jewels.

CALLIOPE

PRESIDED over Eloquence and Heroic
Poetry. She is faid to be the mother of Orpheus by Apollo. Horace fuppofes her to play
on all forts of mufical inftruments. She was
reprefented with books in her hand, which fignified that her office was to take notice of the
famous actions of heroes, as Clio was employed in celebrating them. She held the three
well-known epic Poems of antiquity, and appeared generally crowned with laurel. She
fettled the difpute between Venus and Proferpine concerning Adonis, whofe company
thefe two Goddeffes both wifhed perpetually to
enjoy.

URANIA

URANIA

PRESIDED over Aftronomy. She was the mother of Linus, and fome fay likewife of the God Hymenœus. She was reprefented dreffed in an azure coloured robe, crowned with ftars, holding in her hands a globe, and having many mathematical inftruments placed around her. She is fometimes called the Heavenly Mufe.

Some pretend that there were only three Mufes; Melete, Mneme, and Aœde. Others fay there were four; Talxiope, Aœde, Arche, Melete: they were, according to fome, daughters of Pierus and Antiope, from which circumftance they are often called Pierides; but the name of Pierides might as probably be derived from Mount Pierus, where they were born. They have likewife been called Caftalides, Aganippides, Lebethrides, Aonides, Heliconides, &c. from the places where they were worfhipped, or over which they prefided. Apollo, who was the patron and conductor of the Mufes, has received the name of Mufagetes, or leader of the Mufes; the fame firname was alfo given to Hercules. The palmtree,

tree, the laurel, and all the fountains of Pindus, Helicon, Parnaffas, &c. were facred to the Mufes: they were all fond of folitude, and commonly appeared in different attire, according to the arts and fciences over which they prefided. Sometimes they were reprefented as dancing together, or finging in chorus, to intimate the near and indiffoluble connection which fubfifts between the liberal Arts and Sciences. Sometimes they are feen on mount Parnaffus, or on Mount Helicon, and the horfe Pegafus appears on the fummit, with extended wings, ready to take flight. This horfe is faid to have fprung from the blood of Medufa, when Perfeus had cut off her head; he was called by this name, from his having received exiftence, according to Hefiod, near the fources of the Ocean, from whence he immediately flew up to Heaven; or rather, according to Ovid, he fixed his refidence on Mount Helicon, where, by ftriking the earth with his foot, he inftantly raifed a fountain, which has been named Hippocrene. He became the favourite of the Mufes, and having been tamed by Neptune or Minerva, he was given to Bellerophon to conquer the Chimæra. No fooner was this fiery monfter deftroyed, than Pegafus threw down his rider, becaufe he was a mortal; or rather,

according

according to the more received opinion, becaufe
he attempted to fly to Heaven. This act of
temerity in Bellerophon was punifhed by Jupiter, who fent an infect to torment Pegafus,
which occafioned the melancholy fall of his
rider. Pegafus continued his flight up to
Heaven, and was placed among the conftellations of Jupiter. Perfeus, according to Ovid,
was mounted upon Pegafus, when he deftroyed
the fea-monfter which was going to devour
Andromeda.

The Mufes fometimes appear with wings,
becaufe, by the help of wings, they efcaped
from Pyrenæus, a king of Thrace, who, during a fhower of rain, gave them fhelter in his
houfe, and then attempted to offer them violence. When the Goddeffefs affumed wings, and
flew away, Pyrenæus attempting to follow them
(as if he too had wings), threw himfelf from
the top of a tower, and was killed by the fall.
The nine daughters of Pierus, the Theffalian, who challenged the Mufes by a trial of
fkill in mufic, were conquered by them, and
then changed into magpies. It may therefore
be fuppofed, that the victorious Mufes affumed
the name of the conquered daughters of Pierus,
and that it was for this reafon they were called
Pierides,

Pierides; in the fame manner as Minerva was called Pallas, becaufe fhe had killed the giant of that name. The Mufes were likewife challenged to a trial of fkill by Thamyras, a celebrated mufician of Thrace, and it was mutually agreed, that the vanquifhed fhould be wholly at the difpofal of the victorious adverfary. Thamyras was conquered, and the Mufes deprived him of his fight and his melodious voice, and broke his lyre. The worfhip of the Mufes was well eftablifhed, particularly in the enlightened parts of Greece, Theffaly, and Italy. No facrifices were offered to them, though no poet ever began a poem, without a folemn invocation to thefe Goddeffes. Feftivals were inftituted in honour of them in feveral parts of Greece, efpecially among the Thefpians, every fifth year. The Macedonians alfo obferved a feftival in honour of Jupiter and the Mufes. It had been inftituted by king Archelaus, and it was celebrated with ftage-plays, games, and different exhibitions, which continued nine days, according to the number of the Nine Mufes.

THEMIS,

THEMIS, ASTRÆA, NEMESIS.

———

THEMIS, a daughter of Cœlus and Terra, who was married to Jupiter againſt her incli-nation. She became mother of Dice, Irene, Eunomia, the Parcæ, &c. She was the firſt to whom the inhabitants of the earth raiſed temples. Her Oracle was famous in Attica, in the age of Deucalion, who confulted it with great folemnity, and was inſtructed how to re-pair the lofs of mankind. Themis was gene-rally attended by the Seaſons. Among the moderns ſhe is reprefented as holding a fword in one hand, and a pair of ſcales in the other.

Aſtræa, a daughter of Aſtræus, king of Ar-cadia, or, according to others, of Titan, by Aurora. Some make her the daughter of Ju-piter and Themis. She was called Juſtice, of which virtue ſhe was the Goddefs. She lived upon earth, according to the poets, during the Golden Age ; but the wickednefs and impiety of mankind, in the Brazen and Iron Ages, drove her to Heaven, and ſhe was placed among the

the conftellations in the Zodiac, under the name of Virgo. She is reprefented as a virgin, with a ftern but majeftic countenance, holding, like Themis, a pair of fcales in one hand, and a fword in the other. ☉

Nemefis, the daughter of Nox. She was the Goddefs of Vengeance, always prepared to punifh impiety, and at the fame time liberally to reward the good and virtuous. She is made one of the Parcæ by fome Mythologifts. She was reprefented with a helm and a wheel. The people of Smyrna were the firft who made her ftatues with wings, to fhew with what celerity fhe is prepared to punifh crimes, both by fea and land, as the helm and the wheel in her hands indicate. Her power did not only exift during this life, but fhe was alfo employed, after the death of criminals, to find out the moft effectual and rigorous methods of punifh-ment. Nemefis was particularly worfhiped at Rhamnus, in Attica, where fhe had a cele-brated ftatue ten cubits high, made of Parian marble, by Phidias; or, according to others, by one of his pupils. The·Romans were alfo particularly attached to the adoration of this Deity, whom they folemnly invoked, and to whom they offered facrifices before they de-clared

clared war againſt their enemies, to ſhew the world that their wars were undertaken upon juſt grounds. Her ſtatue at Rome was in the Capitol. Some ſuppoſe that Nemeſis was the perſon whom Jupiter deceived in the form of a ſwan, and that Leda was entruſted with the care of the children which ſprung from the two eggs: others pretend that Leda obtained the name of Nemeſis after death. According to Pauſanias, there was more than one Nemeſis. Goddeſs Nemeſis was ſirnamed Rhamnuſia, be-cauſe worſhiped at Rhamnus; and Adraſtia, from the temple which Adraſtus, king of Argos, erected to her when he went againſt Thebes, to revenge the indignities which his ſon-in-law, Polynices, had ſuffered, in being unjuſtly driven from his kingdom by his brother Eteo-cles. The Greeks celebrated a feſtival, called Nemeſia, in memory of deceaſed perſons, as the Goddeſs Nemeſis was ſuppoſed to defend the relics, and the memory of the dead from all inſult. Nemeſis, though properly one of the infernal Deities, is generally placed among the Terreſtrials, as the third Goddeſs who preſided over juſtice.

THE

THE SYLVAN AND DOMESTIC DEITIES.

PAN	ARISTÆUS
SYLVANUS	TERMINUS
SILENUS	THE SATYRS
PRIAPUS	OR
VERTUMNUS	FAUNS

THE PENATES AND LARES,

THE GENII.

PAN.

—

PAN was the God of Shepherds and Hunters, and of all the inhabitants of the country. He was the son of Mercury by Dryope, according to Homer. Some give him Jupiter and Califto for parents. Others Jupiter and Ybis or Oneis. Lucian, Huginus, &c. fupport that he was the fon of Penelope, the daughter of Icarius, and wife of Ulyffes; but I decline repeating the fhameful and indecent ftories they relate to the prejudice of a Princefs, whom the authority of Homer induces us to regard as a pattern of prudence and chaftity. Pan was a monfter in appearance; he had two fmall horns on his head; his complexion was ruddy, his nofe flat, and his legs, thighs, and feet were thofe of a goat, with the tail of that animal. The education of Pan was entrufted to a nymph of Arcadia, called Sinoe; but the nurfe, terrified at the fight of fuch a monfter, fled away and left him; he was wrapped up in the fkin of a beaft by his father, and carried to Heaven, where Jupiter and the Gods entertained

tained themselves with the oddity of his appearance. Bacchus, who was greatly pleafed with him, gave him the name of Pan. . The God of Shepherds chiefly refided in Arcadia, where the woods and mountains were his habitation. He was faid to have invented the flute with feven reeds, which he called Syrinx; in honour of a beautiful nymph of the fame name, to whom he attempted to offer violence, and who was changed into a reed. He was continually endeavouring to deceive the neighbouring nymphs, and frequently his ftratagems proved fuccefsful. Though deformed in his fhape and features, he had the good fortune to pleafe Diana, and to gain her favour, by transforming himfelf into a beautiful white goat. He was enamoured of a nymph of the mountains, called Echo, by whom · he had a fon, named Lynx. Being in love with Omphale, Queen of Lydia, he went in the night to a cave, to which he knew fhe had retired with Hercules. As they flept in different parts of the cave, and as Omphale had covered herfelf with the fkin of the lion ufually worn by Hercules, Pan miftook her for that hero, and went to the place where Hercules was fleeping, who had affumed the drefs of Omphale, which Pan perceiving, was deceived, and lay down by his fide; but the hero awaking, kicked him

H 2 into

into the middle of the cave.   The noise awoke
Omphale, and Pan was discovered lying on the
ground, greatly disappointed, and ashamed at
his adventure.

The worship of Pan was well established, particularly in Arcadia, where he gave Oracles
on Mount Lycæus.   His festivals, called by
the Greeks Lycæ, were brought to Italy by
Evander, and they were well known at Rome
by the name of the Lupercalia.   The worship, and
the different functions, of this Diety were derived
from the mythology of the ancient Egyptians.
Pan was one of the eight great Gods adored by
this people, who ranked him before the other
twelve, called *Consentes* by the Romans.   He
was worshiped with the greatest solemnity all
over Egypt ; his statutes represented him as a
goat, not because he really was such, but this
was done for mysterious reasons.   He was the
emblem of fecundity, and they looked upon
him as the principle of all things.   His horns,
as some observe, represented the rays of the
sun.   The brightness of the Heavens was ex-
pressed by the vivacity and the ruddiness of his
complexion.   The star which he wore on his
breast was the symbol of the firmament, and
his

his hairy legs and feet denoted the inferior
parts of the earth, covered with woods and
plants. Some fuppofe that Pan appeared as a
goat, becaufe, when the Gods fled into Egypt,
in their war againft the Giants, he transformed
himfelf into that animal. This Deity, according to fome, is the fame as Faunus, and he is
the chief of all the Satyrs. Plutarch mentions, that in the reign of Tiberius, an extraordinary voice was heard near the Echinades,
in the Ionian fea, which exclaimed that the
Great Pan was dead. This was credited by
the emperor, and the aftrologers were confulted; but they were unable to explain the
meaning of fo fupernatural a voice, which probably proceeded from the impofition of one of
the courtiers, who wifhed to terrify Tiberius.
In Egypt, in the town of Mendes (which
word alfo fignifies a goat), there was a facred
goat kept with the moft ceremonious fanctity.
The death of this animal was always attended with the greateft folemnities, and, like
that of Apis, became the caufe of univerfal
mourning. As Pan ufually terrified the inhabitants of the neighbouring country, that kind
of fear which fometimes feizes men, and which
has no real or juft caufe, has been named from

H 3   him

him panic fear. This kind of terror has been examplified, not only in individuals, but alfo in numerous armies; fuch as that of Brennus, which was thrown into the utmoft confternation at Rome, without any caufe or plaufible reafon.

SYLVANUS.

SYLVANUS.

MANY authors confound the Sylvani,
Fauni, and Sileni, with Pan; yet, as others
diftinguifh them, it is neceffary to treat of them
feparately. To begin with Sylvanus; he is
generally placed near Pan, and like him, reprefented as half a man, and half a goat. According to Virgil, he was the fon of Picus, or,
as others report, of Mars. The worfhip of
Sylvanus was eftablifhed only in Italy, where
fome have imagined he reigned in the age of
Evander. This Deity prefided over gardens
and limits. He is reprefented as holding a
branch of cyprefs in his hand, becaufe he was
particularly fond of young Cypariffus, the favourite of Apollo, who was changed into a cyprefs tree.

SILENUS.

SILENUS.

SILENUS was the foster father, the preceptor, and constant attendant of Bacchus. He was, as some suppose, the son of Pan, or, according to others, of Mercury, or of Terra. Malea, in Lesbos, is said to have been the place of his birth. After death he received divine honours, and had a temple in Elis. Silenus is represented as a fat jolly old man, riding on an afs, crowned with flowers, and always intoxicated. He was once found by some peasants in Phrygia, after he had loft his way, and conducted by them to king Midas, who received him hospitably, and afterwards restored him to Bacchus, for which he was rewarded by the God, as has been already related. Some authors affert that Silenus was a philosopher, who accompanied Bacchus in his Indian expedition, and affifted him by his counfels. From this circumstance, therefore, he is fometimes introduced speaking, with all the gravity of a philosopher, concerning the formation of the world, and the nature of things.

PRIAPUS.

PRIAPUS.

PRIAPUS prefided over gardens and orchards. He was fon of Venus by Mercury or
Adonis, or as fome fay, by Bacchus. He was
born at Lampfacus, and was fo deformed in all
his limbs, by means of Juno, who had affifted
at the delivery of Venus, that the mother,
afhamed to have given birth to fuch a monfter,
ordered him to be expofed upon the mountains.
His life, however, was preferved by fhepherds,
and he foon became a favourite of the people of
Lampfacus; but he was afterwards expelled by
the inhabitants, on account of the freedoms he
took with their wives. This violence was punifhed by the fon of Venus; and after the
Lampfacenians had been afflicted with difeafes,
they recalled Priapus and erected temples to his
honour. Feftivals were alfo inftituted, and the
people, naturally indolent and fond of amufe-
ment, gave themfelves up to licentioufnefs, and
every impurity, during the celebration. His
worfhip was alfo introduced at Rome; but the
Romans regarded him rather as the God of

H 5   Gardens

Gardens and Orchards, than as the patron of sensual pleasures. A crown painted with different colours was offered to him in the spring, and, in the summer, a garland of ears of corn. An ass was usually sacrificed to him, because that animal, by its braying, awoke the nymph Lotis, to whom Priapus was going to offer violence. This Deity is generally represented with an human face, and the ears of a goat; he holds a stick in his hand, with which he terrifies the birds, as also a club to drive away thieves, and a scythe to prune the trees, and cut down the corn. He was crowned with the leaves of the vine, and sometimes with laurel, or rocket; the last of these plants is sacred to him, as it is said to raise the passions, and to excite love.

A town of Asia Minor, near Lampsacus, took its name from Priapus, because he was the chief Deity of the place, and because he had taken refuge there, when banished from Lampsacus.

VERTUMNUS.

VERTUMNUS.

A DEITY among the Romans, who prefided over the Spring, and over Orchards. He endeavoured to gain the affections of the Goddefs Pomona; to effect this, he made ufe of the power which he had of affuming many different forms. Some authors fay, that it was under that of an old woman, he prevailed on his miftrefs to liften to his addreffes; but others relate, that having in vain metamorphofed himfelf into a great number of different fhapes, he at laft re-afiumed his own, and Pomona confented to marry him. Vertumnus is reprefented as a handfome young man, crowned with flowers, and holding in his right hand fruit, and a horn of plenty in his left.

ARISTÆUS.

ARISTÆUS, son of Apollo, and the nymph Cyrene, was born in the deserts of Libya. He was brought up by the Seasons, and nourished with Nectar and Ambrosia, the food of the Celestial Gods. His love of hunting procured him the firnames of Nomus and Agreus. After he had travelled over the greatest part of the world, he came to settle in Greece, where he married Autonoe, the daughter of Cadmus, by whom he had a son called Actæon. He was enamoured of Eurydice, the wife of Orpheus, and pursued her in the fields; as she fled from him, she was stung by a serpent that lay in the grass, and died, on which account the Gods destroyed all the bees of Aristæus. In this calamity he applied to his mother, who directed him to seize the Sea-God Proteus, and consult him how he might repair the loss he had sustained. Proteus advised him to appease the manes of Eurydice, by the sacrifice of four bulls, and as many heifers. As soon as he had done so, and left the victims in the open air,

swarms

ſwarms of bees immediately ſprang from the dead carcaſſes, which reſtored Ariſtæus to his former proſperity. Some authors ſay, that this Deity had the care of Bacchus when young, and that he was initiated in all his myſteries. Ariſtæus went to live on mount Haemus, where he was afterwards worſhiped as a Demi-God. He is ſaid to have learned from the Nymphs the cultivation of olives, and the management of bees, &c. which he communicated to mankind.

TERMINUS.

TERMINUS,

A DIVINITY whom the Romans suppofed to prefide over bounds and limits, and to punifh all unlawful ufurpation of land. His worfhip was firft introduced at Rome by Numa, who perfuaded his fubjects that the limits of their lands and eftates were under the immediate infpection of Heaven. His temple was on the Tarpeian Rock. He was reprefented with a human head, without feet or arms, to intimate that he never moved wherever he was placed. The people of the country affembled once a year with their families, and crowned with flowers and garlands, the ftones which feparated their different poffeffions, and offered victims to the God who prefided over their boundaries. It is faid, that when Tarquin the Proud wifhed to build a temple on the Tarpeian Rock to Jupiter, the God Terminus refufed to give way, though the other Gods willingly refigned their feats.

THE

THE SATYRS OR FAUNS.

THEY were Demi-Gods of the country, whofe origin is unknown. They are reprefented as men, but with the feet and legs of goats, fhort horns on the head, and the whole body covered with thick hair: they chiefly attended upon Bacchus, and made themfelves known in his Orgies, by their riotous and lafcivious demeanour. The firft fruits of every thing were generally offered to them. The Romans promifcuoufly called them Fauni, Panes, Sylvani, &c. It is faid that a Satyr was brought to Sylla, as that general returned from Theffaly. The monfter had been furprized afleep in a cave; but his voice was inarticulate when he was brought into the prefence of the Roman general, and Sylla was fo difgufted with it, that he ordered it to be inftantly removed. This monfter anfwered, in every refpect, the defcription which the Poets and Painters have given of the Satyrs.

THE

THE PENATES AND LARES.

T HE Penates, called Houfhold Gods, prefided over houfes and the domeftic affairs of families. They were called Penates, becaufe
they were generally placed in the innermoft and
moft fecret parts of the houfe ; the place where
they ftood was afterwards called Penetralia, and
they themfelves received the name of Penetrales.
It was in the option of every mafter of a family
to choofe his houfehold gods, and therefore Jupiter, and others of the fuperior Gods, are often
invoked as patrons of domeftic affairs. According to fome, the Penates were divided into
four claffes ; the firft comprehended all the Ce-
leftials, the fecond the Sea-Gods, the third the
Gods of Hell, and the laft all fuch heroes as had
received divine honours after death. The Penates were originally the manes of the dead, but
when fuperftition had taught mankind to pay
great reverence to the ftatues and images of
their deceafed friends, this veneration was foon
exchanged for regular worfhip, and they were
admitted by their votaries to fhare immortality
                                        and

and power over the world with a Jupiter or a Minerva. The ſtatues of the Penates were uſually made with wax, ivory, ſilver, or earth, according to the affluence of the worſhipper ; and the offerings they received, were wine, incenſe, fruits, and ſometimes the ſacrifice of lambs, ſheep, goats, &c. In the early ages of Rome, human ſacrifices were offered to them ; but Brutus, who expelled the Tarquins, aboliſhed that unnatural cuſtom. When offerings were made to the Penates, their ſtatues were crowned with garlands, poppies, or garlick ; and beſides the monthly day that was ſet apart for their worſhip, their feſtivals were celebrated during the Saturnalia.

THE LARES

WERE Gods of inferior power, who likewiſe preſided over houſes and families. They were two in number, ſons of Mercury and the Nymph Lara, who was famous for her beauty and her loquacity ; having revealed to Juno the amours of Jupiter with Juturna, the God cut off her tongue, and ordered Mercury to conduct

conduct her to the infernal regions. The Meffenger of the Gods fell in love with her by the
way, and Lara became, in confequence of this
amour, the mother of two children, to whom
the Romans have fince paid divine honours,
under the name of Lares.   In procefs of time
their power was extended not only over houfes,
but alfo over the country and the fea; and we
find Lares Urbani, to prefide over the cities;
Familiares, over houfes; Ruftici, over the
country; Compitales, over crofs-ways; Ma-
rini, over the Sea; Viales, over the roads, &c.
According to the opinion of fome, the worfhip
of the Gods Lares, whom they fuppofe to be
the Manes, arifes from the ancient cuftom
among the Romans and other nations, of bury-
ing their dead in their houfes, and from the belief that their fpirit continually hovered over the
houfe for the protection of its inhabitants.   The
ftatues of the Lares refembling monkies, and
covered with the fkin of a dog, were placed in
a niche behind the doors of the houfes, or
around the hearths.   At the feet of the Lares
was the figure of a dog barking, to intimate
their care and vigilance.   Incenfe was burnt
on their altars, and a fow was alfo offered
on particular days.   Their feftivals were obferved

ferved at Rome in the month of May, when their ftatues were crowned with garlands of flowers, and offerings of fruit were prefented to them. The word Lares fignifies Conductor or Leader.

THE

THE GENII

WERE beings of a middle kind, of greater dignity than man, but of a nature inferior to that of the Gods. According to the Ancients, they were fpirits or Dæmons which prefided over the birth and life of every man, gave them their private counfels, and carefully watched over their moft fecret intentions. Some of the ancient Philofophers maintained that every man had two of thefe Dæmons, the one good and the other bad. They were fuppofed to have the power of affuming whatever forms were moft fubfervient to their defigns. At the moment of death, the Dæmon delivered up to judgment the perfon with whofe care he had been entrufted; and, according to the evidence he gave, fentence was paffed upon the deceafed. The Dæmon of Socrates is famous in hiftory. That great Philofopher afferted, that the Genius informed him when any one of his friends was about to engage in fome unfortunate enterprize, and prevented

himfelf

himfelf from the commiffion of all crimes and impiety. Thefe Genii or Dæmons, though at firft reckoned only as fubordinate minifters of the fuperior Deities, received divine honours in procefs of time, and altars and ftatues were erected to them.

THE SYLVAN GODDESSES.

| PALES | TERONIA |
| FLORA | FOMONA |

THE NYMPHS AND THE SIBYLS.

PALES.

———

THE Goddess of sheep-folds and of pastures among the Romans. She was worshipped with great solemnity, and her festivals, called Palilia, were celebrated the very day that Romulous began to lay the foundation of the city of Rome. These feasts were instituted to engage the Goddess to make the pastures fruitful, and to preserve the flocks from wolves, and from the diseases incident to cattle. They offered to her milk, and wafers made with millet. Pales is represented as an aged woman, surrounded by shepherds.

FLORA.

FLORA.

THE Goddefs of flowers and gardens among the Romans. She is the fame as the Chloris of the Greeks. Some fuppofe that she was originally a courtezan, who left to the Romans the immenfe riches which she had acquired by her irregularities, in remembrance of which a yearly feftival was inftituted in honour of Flora ; but she was worshiped among the Sabines long before the foundation of Rome, and Tatius was the firft who raifed her a temple in that city. It is faid that she married Zephyrus, and received from him the privileges of prefiding over flowers, and of enjoying perpetual youth. She was reprefented as crowned with flowers, and holding in her hand the horn of plenty.

FERONIA.

FERONIA.

A Goddefs at Rome, who prefided over woods and groves. The name is perhaps derived from the town Feronia, near Mount Soracte, where fhe had a Temple. It was ufual to make a yearly facrifice to her, and to wafh the face and hands in the waters of the facred fountain which flowed near her Temple. It is faid that thofe filled with the fpirit of this Goddefs could walk bare-footed over burning coals without receiving any injury. It has been likewife related, that the facred grove in which her Temple ftood having been fet on fire, the votaries of Feronia were about to remove her image from thence, when on a fudden the grove became green as before.

POMONA.

POMONA.

A Nymph, fuppofed by the Romans to prefide over gardens, and to be the Goddefs of all
forts of fruit-trees. She had a Temple at
Rome, and a regular Prieft, who offered facrifices to her divinity for the prefervation of
fruit. She was reprefented fitting on a bafket
full of flowers and fruits, holding a bough in
one hand, and apples in the other. Pomona
was fond of the cultivation of the earth, and
difregarded the fports of the field. Many of
the rural Gods endeavoured to gain her affection, but fhe received the addreffes of them all
with equal coldnefs, till Vertumnus, by affuming different fhapes, introduced himfelf into her
retreat, and prevailed on her to efpoufe him.
This Deity was unknown among the Greeks.

THE NYMPHS.

CERTAIN female Deities among the ancients. They were generally divided into two classes, Nymphs of the Land, and Nymphs of the Sea. Of the Nymphs of the Earth, some presided over the woods, and were ca lde Dryades, and Hamodryades; others presided over mountains, and were called Oreades; and others over hills and vallies, and were called Napææ, &c. The Sea-Nymphs were the Oceanides, and Nereides; and those who presided over rivers, fountains, streams, and lakes, were called Naiades, Potamides, &c. The Nymphs of the Waters generally inhabited the element to which they belonged, and those of the land fixed their residence on rocks, or mountains, in woods or caverns, and their grottos were beautified by evergreens, and delightful romantic scenes. The Nymphs were immortal according to some Mythologists; others supposed that they were subject to mortality, but that their life was of long duration. According to Hesiod, they lived several thou-

sand

fand years; and Plutarch feems obfcurely to intimate, that the term of their life was about 9720 years. The number of the Nymphs is not precifely known; there were above 3000 according to Hefiod; whofe power was extended over the different parts of the earth, and over the different functions and occupations of mankind. They were worfhiped by the Ancients, though not with fo much folemnity as the fuperior Deities. They had no temples raifed to their honour, and the only offerings they received were milk, honey and oil, and fometimes the facrifice of a goat. They were reprefented as young and beautiful virgins, veiled up to the middle; they fometimes held a vafe, from which they feemed to pour water. Sometimes they held grafs, leaves, and fhells inftead of vafes. It was deemed unfortunate to fee them naked, and fuch a fight was ufually attended by an immediate delirium. The Nymphs were generally diftinguifhed by an epithet which denoted the place of their refidence. Thus the Nymphs of Sicily were called Sicilides, thofe of Corycus, Corycides, &c.

Echo is faid to have been formerly one of the Nymphs, though nothing but her voice now remains, and even while fhe lived, fhe was fo

far

far deprived of the use of speech, as not to
be able to repeat the last words of any sentence.
Juno had inflicted this punishment on her for
her loquacity. Echo accidentally met in the
woods, Narcissus, a beautiful youth, son of
Cephisus and the Nymph Liriope, and fell pas-
sionately in love with him. She discovered her
fondness to him, but he despised her and fled
from her sight, at which the Nymph was so
much afflicted, that she pined away with grief,
till every part of her was consumed except her
voice, which still haunts the woods and mountains which she once frequented, and repeats,
though imperfectly, the sounds which are heard
among them. Narcissus, after he had fled from
Echo, stopped to repose himself by the side of a
fountain, where seeing his own image re-
flected, he became deeply enamoured of it,
taking it for the Nymph of the place; his fruit-
less attempts to approach this beautiful object
so enraged him, that he grew desperate and
killed himself, and his blood was changed into
a flower, which still bears his name.

THE SIBYLS.

THE Sibyls were certain women, infpired by Heaven, who flourifhed in different parts of the world. Their number is unknown. Plato fpeaks of one only, others of two, Pliny of three, Ælian of four, and Varro of ten; an opinion which is univerfally adopted by the learned. Thefe ten Sibyls were believed to refide in the following places, Perfia, Libya, Delphi, Cumæ, in Italy, Erythræa, Cumæ, in Æolia, Marpeffa on the Hellefpont, Ancyra, in Phrygia, and Tiburtis. The moft celebrated of the Sibyls was that of Cumæ, in Italy, who has been called by the different names of Amalthæa, Demophile, Herophile, Daphne, Manto, Phemonoe, and Deiphobe. It is faid that Apollo became enamoured of her; and that to make her fenfible to his paffion, he offered to grant her whatever fhe fhould afk. The Sibyl demanded to live as many years as fhe then held grains of fand in her hand, which was full of them; but fhe forgot to afk, at the fame time, for the continuance of the health, vigour, and

I 4 bloom

bloom of which fhe was then in poffeffion. The
God granted her requeft; but fhe ftill refufed
to gratify his paffion, though he even offered
her perpetual youth and beauty on that condition.   She became at length old and decrepit;
her form decayed, melancholy palenefs, and
haggard looks, fucceeded to bloom and cheer-
fulnefs.   She had already lived about 700 years
when Æneas arrived in Italy; and, as fome
have imagined, fhe had three centuries more to
live,- before her years became as numerous as
the grains of fand which had been contained in
her hand. This Sibyl inftructed Æneas how
to find his father in the infernal regions, and
even conducted him to the entrance of Hell. It
was ufual for the Sibyl to write her prophecies
on leaves, which fhe placed at the entrance of
her cave; and it required particular care in
thofe who confulted her to take up thefe leaves
before they were difperfed by the wind, as their
meaning then became incomprehenfible.   According to the moft authentic hiftorians of the
Roman Republic, one of the Sibyls came to
the palace of Tarquin the Second with nine
volumes, which fhe offered to fell for a very high
price. The monarch difregarded her, and fhe
immediately difappeared; but foon after, having
burned three of the volumes, fhe afked the
price

price for the remaining fix books; and when Tarquin refufed to buy them, fhe burned three more, and ftill perfifted in demanding the fame fum for the three that-were left. This extra-ordinary behaviour aftonifhed Tarquin; he purchafed the books, and the Sibyl inftantly va-nifhed, and never more appeared to the world. Thefe books were preferved with great care, and called the Sibylline verfes. A college of priefts was appointed to have the care of them; and fuch reverence did the Romans entertain for thefe prophetic books, that they were con-fulted with the greateft folemnity, and only when the ftate feemed to be in danger. When the capitol was burnt in the troubles of Sylla, the Sibylline verfes, which were depofited there, perifhed in the conflagration; and to repair the lofs which the Republic was thought to have fuftained, commiffioners were fent immediately to different parts of Greece, to collect whatever verfes could be found of the infpired writings of the Sibyls. The fate of thefe Sibylline verfes, which were collected after the conflagration of the capitol, is unknown. There are now many Sibylline verfes extant, but they are univerfally accounted fpurious; and, it is evident, that they were compofed in the fecond century, by fome of the followers of Chriftianity, who

wifhed

wished to convince the Pagans of their errors, by assisting the cause of truth with the arms of pious artifice.

There were many inferior Gods and Goddesses adored by the Ancients, besides those which have been here mentioned; in effect they are almost innumerable, as almost every part of the world invoked a great number of Divinities which were unknown among other nations. The same Deities were indeed acknowledged in many different countries, but under different appellations, and different powers and functions were ascribed to them; but some of those functions were so absurd, and others so indecent, that I have thought it best to pass many of them over in silence, and proceed to those whose actions make a more essential part of the fabulous history.

THE

THE MARINE DEITIES.

NEPTUNE	TETHYS
TRITON	AMPHITRITE
OCEANUS	DORIS
NEREUS	THETIS
PROTEUS	LEUCOTHEA
GLAUCUS	AND PALÆMON.

MONSTERS OF THE SEA,

THE SIRENS,

SCYLLA AND CHARYBDIS.

NEPTUNE.

NEPTUNE, son of Saturn and Ops, and brother to Jupiter and Pluto. He was preserved in the same manner with them from being devoured by his father, on the day of his birth. Neptune shared with his brothers the empire of Saturn, and received as his portion the dominion of the sea. This, however, did not seem to him equivalent to the empire of Heaven and Earth, of which Jupiter had taken possession; he therefore conspired, with others of the Gods, to dethrone him. The conspiracy was discovered, and Neptune was condemned by Jupiter to build the walls of Troy. A reconciliation, however, soon took place, and Neptune was re-instated in all his rights and privileges. His dispute with the Goddess Minerva has been already taken notice of. The decision which was given in her favour, had highly offended Neptune, and he afterwards contended with her for Trœzene; but Jupiter composed that difference, by permitting them to be conjointly worshiped there, and by

giving

giving the name of Polias, or Protectress of the
city, to Minerva, and that of king of Trœzene,
to the God of the Sea. He likewise disputed
for the Iftmus of Corinth with Apollo; and
Briareus, the Cyclop, who was mutually chosen
umpire, gave the Iftmus to Neptune, and the
promontory to Apollo. Neptune, as being
God of the Sea, was entitled to more power
than any of the other Gods, except Jupiter.
Not only the ocean, rivers, and fountains, were
subjected to him, but he could also raise earth-
quakes at his pleafure, and bring up iflands from
the bottom of the sea, with a ftroke of his
trident.

The worfhip of Neptune was eftablifhed in
almoft all parts of the earth, and the Lybians in
particular venerated him above all other nations, and even confidered him as the firft and
greateft of the Gods. The Greeks and Romans were alfo much attached to his worfhip,
and they celebrated their Iftmian games and
confualia with the greateft folemnity. Neptune was generally reprefented fitting in a chariot made of a fhell, and drawn by fea-horfes or
dolphins. Sometimes he is drawn by winged
horfes, and ftands up holding his trident, while
his chariot flies over the furface of the waves.
Homer

Homer reprefents him as iffuing from the fea, and in three fteps croffing the whole horizon. The mountains and the forefts, fays the poet, in his defcription, tremble as he walks; the whales, and all the fifhes of the fea appear around him, and even the fea herfelf feems to feel the prefence of her God. The Ancients generally facrificed a bull and a horfe on his altars, and the Roman foothfayers always offered to him the gall of the victims, which, in tafte, refembles the bitternefs of the fea-water.

The amours of Neptune were numerous. He obtained, by means of a dolphin, the favour of Amphitrite, who had made a vow of perpetual celibacy, and he placed among the conftellations the fifh which had prevailed upon the Goddefs to become his wife; he alfo married Venilia and Salacia, but thefe, according to fome authors, are only the names of Amphitrite; they obferve that the former word is derived from *Venire*, alluding to the continual motion of the fea. Salacia is derived from *Salum*, which fignifies the fea, and is applicable to Amphitrite. Neptune affumed the form of the river Enipeus, to gain the confidence of Tyro, the daughter of Salmoneus, by whom he had Pelias and Neleus; he was alfo father of Pho-

reus

reus and Poliphemus, by Thooffa; of Lycus, Nycteus and Euphemus, by Celeno; of
Chryfes, by Chryfogenia; of Anœus, by Afty-
palia; of Bœotus and Hellen, by Antiope; of
Lucanoe, by Themefto; of Agenor and Bellerophon, by Eurynome, the daughter of Ny-
fus; of Antas, by Alcyone, the daughter of
Atlas; of Abas, by Arethufa; of Actor and
Dictys, by Agemede, the daughter of Augias;
of Megareus, by Œnope, daughter of Epo-
peus; of Cycnus, by Harpalyce; of Tarus,
Otus, Ephialtes, Dorus, Alefus, &c. Neptune
was likewife faid to be father of the horfe Arion,
which had the power of fpeech, by Ceres; and
of the ram with the golden fleece, which carried Phryxus to Colchis, by Theophane, a
daughter of Bifaltus.

The word Neptune is often ufed metaphorically by the poets, to fignify fea-water. In
the Confualia of the Romans, horfes were led
through the ftreets richly caparifoned, and
crowned with garlands; as the God, in whofe
honour thofe feftivals were inftituted, had produced the horfe, an animal fo beneficial to
mankind.

TRITON.

TRITON,

SON of Neptune, by Amphitrite, or, according to some, by Celeno, or Salacia. He was very powerful among the Sea-Deities, and could calm the sea, and abate storms at pleasure. He is generally represented as blowing a shell. His body above the waist is like that of a man, and below like a dolphin. Some represent him with the fore-feet of a horse. Many of the Sea-Deities are called Tritons, but the name is usually applied to those only who are half men, and half fishes.

OCEANUS

WAS another powerful Deity of the fea, fon of Cœlus and Terra. He married Tethys, by whom he had the rivers Alpheus, Peneus, Strymon, &c. with a great number of daughters, who were called from him Oceanides. According to Homer, Oceanus was the father of all the Gods, and, on that account, he received frequent vifits from them. He is reprefented as an old man with a long flowing beard, and fitting upon the waves of the fea; he often holds a pike in his hand, and fhips under fail appear at a diftance, or a fea-monfter is feen near him. Oceanus prefided over every part of the fea; and even the rivers were fubject to his power. The ancients were fuperftitious in their worfhip of Oceanus, and revered with great folemnity a Deity, to whofe care they entrufted themfelves when going on any voyage.

NEREUS,

NEREUS,

SON of Oceanus and Terra. He married Doris, by whom he had fifty daughters, which were the Nymphs called Nereides. Nereus was represented as an old man with a long beard, and hair of an azure colour. The chief place of his residence was in the Ægean Sea, where he was surrounded by his daughters, who often formed dances around him. He had the gift of prophecy, and informed those who consulted him with the fates that attended them. He acquainted Paris with the consequence of his elopement with Helen, and it was by his directions, that Hercules obtained the golden apples of the Hesperides; but the Sea-God often evaded the importunities of enquirers, by assuming different shapes, and escaping from their grasp. The word Nereus is sometimes taken for the sea itself. Nereus is called by some the most ancient of all the Gods.

PROTEUS.

PROTEUS,

SON of Oceanus and Tethys, or, according
to some, of Neptune and Phœnice. He had
received the gift of prophecy from Neptune;
and from his knowledge of futurity, mankind
derived the moft important advantages. He
ufually refided in the Carpathian fea; and frequently repofed himfelf upon the fea-fhore,
where fuch as wifhed to confult him reforted.
He was difficult of accefs, and when confulted,
frequently eluded giving the anfwers required,
by immediately affuming, like Nereus, different
forms, and making his efcape, if not well fecured by fetters, during his repofe. Ariftæus
was in the number of thofe who confulted him,
as alfo was Hercules. Some fuppofe that Proteus
was originally a king of Egypt, known among
his fubjects by the name of Cetes; and they
affert that he had two fons, Telegonus and Po-
lygonus, who were both killed by Hercules.
He had alfo fome daughters, among whom were
Cabira, Eridothea, and Rhetea.

GLAUCUS.

GLAUCUS

WAS a fisherman of Anthedon, in Bœotia. He was by some, reputed the son of Neptune and Nais, and by others, of Mercury. As he was fishing, he observed that all the fishes which he laid on the grass received fresh vigour as they touched the ground, and immediately escaped from him, by leaping again into the sea; he attributed the cause of this to the grass, and by tasting it, he found himself suddenly moved with a desire of living in the sea, upon which he leaped into the water, and was made a Sea-Deity by Oceanus and Tethys. After this transformation he became enamoured of the Nereid Scylla, who was so severely punished by Circe. Glaucus is represented like the other Sea-Deities, with a long beard, dishevelled hair, and shaggy eye-brows, and with the tail of a fish. He received the gift of prophecy from Apollo, and he was, according to some, the interpreter of Nereus. He assisted the Argonauts in their expedition, and foretold to them that Hercules

and

and the two fons of Leda would one day receive immortal honours. The fable of his
metamorphofis has been explained by fome authors, who obferve, that he was an excellent
diver, who was devoured by fifhes as he was
fwimming in the fea.

TETHYS,

ONE of the greateſt of the Sea Deities, the wife of Oceanus, and daughter of Uranus and Terra. She was the mother of the principal rivers of the Univerſe, and of the Oceanides. Tethys is confounded by ſome Mythologiſts, with her grand-daughter Thetis. The word Tethys is poetically uſed to exprefs the ſea.

AMPHITRITE.

AMPHITRITE, daughter of Oceanus and Tethys, the wife of Neptune, and mother of Triton. She had a ſtatue at Corinth in the Temple of Neptune. She is ſometimes called Salacia, and is often taken for the ſea itſelf.

DORIS,

DORIS.

DORIS, another of the Oceanides. She married her brother Nerus, and was the Mother of the Nereides. Her name is likewife fometimes ufed to exprefs the fea itfelf.

THETIS.

THETIS, daughter of Nereus and Doris. She was beloved by Jupiter and Neptune; but as the Fates had ordained that the fon fhe fhould bring forth muft become greater than his father, both Gods withdrew their addreffes, and Peleus, the fon of Æacus, was allowed to folicit her hand. Thetis refufed him, but the lover had the artifice to catch her when afleep, and by binding her ftrongly, he prevented her from efcaping. When Thetis found that fhe could not elude the vigilance of her lover, fhe

consented

confented to marry him, though with much reluctance. Their nuptials were celebrated on Mount Pelion with great pomp. All the Deities attended, except the Goddefs of Difcord, who had not been invited; and who in revenge for this neglect, threw into the midft of the affembly the golden apple which proved fo fatal to Paris and to Troy. Thetis became mother of feveral children by Peleus, but fhe deftroyed them by fire, in order to prove if they were immortal. Achilles muft have fhared the fame fate, if Peleus had not fnatched him from her hand as fhe was going to repeat the cruel operation. She afterwards rendered him invulnerable, by plunging him in the waters of the Styx, except that part of the heel by which fhe held him. As Thetis well knew the fate which attended her fon, fhe endeavoured to keep him from the Trojan war, by concealing him in the Court of Lycomedes, but it was in vain, and he went with the reft of the Greeks. The mother ftill anxious for his prefervation, prevailed upon Vulcan to make him a fuit of armour. When Achilles was killed by Paris, Thetis iffued out of the fea, with the Nereides, to mourn his death; and after fhe had collected his afhes in a golden urn, fhe raifed a monument to his memory, and inftituted feftivals in his honour.

LEUCOTHEA

LEUCOTHEA AND PALÆMON.

INO, and her son Melicerta were transformed into Sea Deities by Neptune, and assumed the Names of Lucothea and Palæmon. Their story has been related under the article of Juno.

THE SIRENS.

THEY were Nymphs of the Sea, who, by their melodious voice, charmed their hearers so much, that they forgot every thing to listen to them ; and after having lulled them to sleep, these monsters devoured them. They were daughters of the Archelous, by the Muse Calliope ; or, according to others, Melpomene, or Terpsichore. They were three in number ;

K   Parthenope,

Parthenope, Ligeia, and Leucofia, and ufually
refided in a fmall ifland, near the Cape Pelorus
in Sicily. Some authors defcribe them as monfters which had the body of a woman above
the waift, and the reft of the body like that of a
bird; or rather that the whole body was covered with feathers, and had the fhape of a bird,
except the head, which was that of a beautiful
female. This monftrous form they had received from Ceres, to punifh them, becaufe they
had not affifted her daughter when fhe was carried away by Pluto. But according to Ovid,
they were fo difconfolate on account of the rape
of Proferpine, that they prayed the Gods to
give them wings, that they might feek her both
by fea and land. The Sirens were informed
by an oracle, that fo foon as any perfon fhould
pafs by them, without fuffering himfelf to be
charmed by their fongs, they fhould perifh;
and their melody had prevailed in attracting all
paffengers to their ruin, till Ulyffes, warned by
Circe of the power of their voice, ftopped the
ears of his companions with wax, and ordered
himfelf to be bound to the maft of his fhip, en-
joining that no attention fhould be paid to his
commands, fhould he wifh to ftay and liften to
the fong. This was a falutary precaution.
Ulyffes made figns to his companions to ftop,
but

but they were difregarded, and the fatal coaft
was paffed with fafety. The Sirens were fo
enraged and difappointed by the fuccefs of this
artifice of Ulyffes, that they threw themfelves
into the fea, and were turned to ftones. Orpheus is faid to have evaded likewife the temp-
tations of the Sirens ; but this was by overcom-
ing them in their own art, and by playing upon
his harp, and finging fo well, that they were
charmed in their turn, and rendered incapable
of doing him any injury. Some authors fay,
that the Sirens had challenged the Mufes to a
trial of fkill in finging ; and that the latter prov-
ing victorious, plucked the feathers from
the wings of their adverfaries, with which they
made themfelves crowns. The place where
the Sirens perifhed was afterwards called
Sirenis, on the coaft of Sicily. Some fuppofe that the Sirens were women who profti-
tuted themfelves to ftrangers, and made them
forget their purfuits, while drowned in unlawful pleafures. They are often reprefented holding one a lyre, a fecond a flute, and the third
finging.

SCYLLA.

SCYLLA, a daughter of Typhon ; or, as some say, of Phorcis. She rejected the addresses of Glaucus ; and the God, to render her more propitious, applied to Circe, whose knowledge of herbs and incantations was universally admired. Circe no sooner saw him, than she became enamoured of him ; and instead of giving him the required assistance, she attempted to make him forget Scylla, but in vain. To punish her rival, Circe poured the juice of some poisonous herbs into the waters of a fountain where Scylla usually bathed herself ; and no sooner had the Nymph entered it, than she found every part of her body below the waist changed into frightful monsters like dogs, which never ceased barking. The rest of her body assumed an equally hideous form. She found herself supported by twelve feet, and she had six different heads, each with three rows of teeth. This sudden and dreadful metamorphosis filled her with such horror, that she threw herself into that part of the sea which seperates

the

the coast of Italy and Sicily; where she was
changed into rocks, which continued to bear
her name, and which was universally deemed
very dangerous to navigators. This Scylla
has been often confounded with another Scylla,
who was the daughter of Nisus, King of Megara, and who was changed into a lark.

CHARYBDIS.

CHARYBDIS.

IT is fuppofed that fhe was an avaricious woman, who ftole the Oxen of Hercules ; for
which theft fhe was ftruck with thunder by Jupiter, and changed into a whirlpool, which is
oppofite the rocks of Scylla, and is likewife extremely dangerous to mariners. It proved fatal
to part of the fleet of Ulyffes. The proverb—

In avoiding Scylla, we may fall into Charybdis—

Shews, that in our eagernefs to avoid one evil,
we fometimes expofe ourfelves to a greater.

Virgils defcription of thefe two monfters is fo
beautiful, and gives fo perfect an idea of the
opinions of the Ancients concerning them, that
I cannot forbear inferting it.

Far on the right her dogs foul Scylla hides :
Charybdis roaring on the left prefides,
And in her greedy whirlpool fucks the tides :

Then

Then fpouts them from below ; with fury driv'n,
The waves mount up, and wafh the face of heaven:
But Scylla, from her den, with open jaws
The finking veffel in her eddy draws,
Then dafhes on the rocks : a human face,
And virgin-bofom, hides the tail's difgrace.
Her parts obfcene below the waves defcend,
With dogs inclos'd, and in a dolphin end.

DRYDEN's VIRGIL, ÆNEID, BOOK III.

K 4

THE INFERNAL DEITIES.

PLUTO	THE FURIES
PLUTUS	NIGHT
PROSERPINE	DEATH
THE FATES	AND SLEEP.

JUDGES OF HELL,

THE MOST FAMOUS OF THE
CONDEMNED IN HELL,

MONSTERS OF HELL,

CHARON AND CERBERUS.

RIVERS OF HELL,

TARTARUS, ELYSIUM.

PLUTO.

—

PLUTO, fon of Saturn and Ops, inherited his father's kingdom with his brothers Jupiter and Neptune. He received, as his lot, the empire of Hell, and whatever lies under the earth; he was therefore called, the God of the Infernal Regions, of death and funerals. From his functions, and the place which he inhabited, he received different appellations. He is commonly ſtiled the Infernal Jupiter; he is alſo called Dis, Hades or Ades, Clytopolon, Agelaſtus, Orcus, &c. As the place of his reſidence was obſcure and gloomy, all the Goddeſſes refuſed to marry him; but he determined to obtain by force, what was denied to his ſolicitations. As he once viſited the iſland of Sicily, after a violent earthquake, he ſaw Proſerpine, the daughter of Ceres, gathering flowers in the plains of Enna, with a crowd of female attendants; he became enamoured of her, and immediately carried her away in his chariot, drawn by four black horſes. To conceal his retreat the more effectually, he opened himſelf a paſſage through the

the earth, by ftriking it with his trident, in the lake of Cyane, in Sicily; or, according to others, on the borders of the Cephifus, in Attica. Proferpine called upon her attendants for help, but it was in vain: they were unable to afford her any, and fhe became the wife of her ravifher, and the queen of Hell. Pluto is generally reprefented holding a trident with two teeth; he has alfo keys in his hands, to intimate, that whoever enters his kingdom, can never return from it. He is looked upon as a cruel and inexorable Deity, and therefore appears with a grim and difmal afpect: for this reafon no temples were raifed to his honour, as to the reft of the fuperior Gods. Black victims, particularly a bull, were the only facrifices which were offered to him, and their blood was not fprinkled on the altars, or received in veffels as at other facrifices; but it was permitted to run down into the earth, as if it were to penetrate as far as the realms of the God. The Syracufans yearly facrificed black bulls to him near the fountain of Cyane; where, according to the received traditions, he had difappeared with Proferpine. Among plants, the cyprefs, the narciffus, and the maiden-hair, were facred to him, as alfo every thing which was deemed inaufpicious, particularly the number

K 6   two.

two. According to some of the Ancients, Pluto sat on a throne of sulphur, from which issued the rivers of Lethe, Cocytus, Phlegethon, and Acheron. The dog Cerberus watched at his feet. The Harpies hovered around him. Proserpine sat on his left hand, and near the Goddess stood the Eumenides, with their heads covered with snakes. The Parcæ occupied the right, and they held in their hands the symbols, each of their respective office, the distaff, the spindle, and the scissars. Pluto is called by some the father of the Eumenides. During the war of the Gods with the Titans, the Cyclops fabricated a helmet, which rendered the wearer invisible, and gave it to Pluto. Perseus was armed with it when he conquered the Gorgons.

PLUTUS.

PLUTUS.

PLUTUS, fon of Jafion, or Jafius, by Ceres, has been confounded with Pluto by many Mythologifts, though plainly diftinguifhed from him, as being the God of Riches. He was brought up by the Goddefs of Peace; and on that account Pax was reprefented at Athens as holding the God of Wealth in her lap. The Greeks regarded him as a capricious Deity; they reprefented him as blind, becaufe he diftributed riches indifcriminately; he was lame, becaufe he arrived by flow and gradual degrees; but he had wings, to intimate that he flew away with more velocity than he approached. Plutus is placed among the Infernal Gods, becaufe the riches which men fo eagerly defire, muft be fought for in the bowels of the earth; and becaufe in the purfuit of them, they are frequently induced to commit crimes, which conduct them finally to the Infernal Regions.

PROSERPINE.

PROSERPINE.

PROSERPINE, the daughter of Ceres, by
Jupiter; she is called by the Greeks, Perse-
phone; she was extremely beautiful, and was,
as been related, carried away by Pluto into the
infernal regions, of which she became the
queen; as such, and as the wife of Pluto, Proserpine presided over the death of mankind, and,
according to the opinion of the Ancients, no
one could die unless the Goddess herself, or
Atropos her minister, cut off one of the hairs
from the head.   From this superstitious belief,
it was usual to cut off some of the hair of the
deceased, and to strew it before the door of the
house, as an offering to Proserpine. The Sicilians
were very particular in their worship to this
Goddess; and, as they believed that the fountain
Cyane had risen from the earth at the very
place where Pluto had opened himself a pas-
sage, they annually sacrificed there a bull, of
which they suffered the blood to flow into the
waters.   Proserpine was universally worshiped
by the Ancients, and she was known by the different

ferent names of Core, Theogamia, Libitina, Hecate, Juno Inferna, Anthefphoria, Cotyto, Deois, Libera, &c. It is faid that Proferpine loved her difagreeable hufband fo much, that fhe was jealous of Mentha, who was his miftrefs, and changed her into an herb called Mint, from her name.

THE FATES.

THE Fates were powerful Goddeſſes, who preſided over the birth, life, and death, of mankind. They were three in number, Clotho, Lacheſis, and Atropos, daughters of Nox and Erebus, according to Heſiod; and of Jupiter and Themis, according to the ſame poet in another poem; and ſome make them daughters of the Sea. Clotho, the youngeſt of the ſiſters, preſided over the moment of birth, and held a diſtaff in her hand. Lacheſis ſpun out all the events and actions of human life; and, finally, Atropos cut the thread of it with a pair of ſciſſars. The power of the Parcæ was great and extenſive. Some ſuppoſe that they were ſubjected to none of the Gods except Jupiter; while others maintain, that even Jupiter himſelf was obedient to their decrees; and, in effect, we ſee the father of the Gods, in Homer's Iliad, unwilling to ſee Patroclus periſh, yet obliged by the ſuperior power of the Fates to abandon him to his deſtiny. According to the moſt received opinions, they were the arbiters of the life and

death

death of mankind, and whatever good or evil befel them in the world, immediately proceeded from the Fates. Some make them the ministers of the king of Hell, and represent them sitting at the foot of his throne. Others represent them as placed on radiant thrones amidst the celestial spheres, cloathed in robes spangled with stars, and wearing crowns on their heads. According to Pausanius, the names of the Parcæ were different from those already mentioned. The most ancient of all, as the Geographer observes, was Venus Urania, who presided over the birth of men; the second was Fortune; and Ilithyia was the third. To these some add a fourth, Proserpina, who often disputes with Atropos the right of cutting the thread of human life. The worship of the Parcæ was well established in some cities of Greece, and though mankind believed them inexorable, and that it was impossible to mitigate them, yet they were willing to shew a proper respect of their Divinity, by raising them temples and statues. They received the same worship as the Furies, and their votaries annually sacrificed to them black sheep; during which solemnity, the priests were crowned with garlands of flowers. The Parcæ were generally represented as three old women, with

chaplets

chaplets made of wool, and interwoven with the flower called narciffus:—they were feen cloathed in white robes, but their drefs is differently defcribed by different authors. According to fome, Clotho has a variegated robe, and on her head a crown of feven ftars. She holds a diftaff in her hand, reaching from Heaven to Earth. The robe worn by Lachefis is variegated with a great number of ftars, and near her are placed a variety of fpindles. Atropos is cloathed in black, and holds fciffars in her hand, with clues of thread of different fizes, according to the length of the lives whofe deftinies they feem to contain. The Fates are called the Secretaries of Heaven, and the guardians of the archives of Eternity.

THE

THE FURIES.

THE Furies were called Eumenides by the Ancients : they were faid to fpring from the blood of a wound which Cœlus received from his fon Saturn. According to others, they were daughters of the Earth, and conceived from the blood of Saturn ; and fome make them daughters of Acheron and Night, or of Pluto and Proferpine. According to the moft received opinions, they were three in number, Tifiphone, Megara, and Alecto, to which fome add Nemefis. Plutarch mentions only one called Adrafta, daughter of Jupiter and Neceffity : they were fuppofed to be the minifters of the vengeance of the Gods; they were ftern and inexorable, and were conftantly employed in punifhing the guilty upon earth, as well as in the infernal regions; they inflicted vengeance upon earth by wars, peftilence, and diffentions, and by the fecret ftings of confcience ; and in in Hell they punifhed the guilty by continual flagellation and torments; they were alfo called Furiae and Erinuyes : their worfhip was almoft

moſt univerſal, and people dared not to mention their names, or to fix their eyes upon their
temples: they were honoured with ſacrifices
and libations; and in Achaia they had a temple,
which, when entered by any criminal perſon,
ſuddenly rendered him furious, and deprived
him of the uſe of his reaſon. In the ſacrifices,
the votaries uſed branches of cedar, and of
alder, hawthorn, ſaffron, and juniper; and the
victims were generally turtle doves and ſheep,
with libations of wine and honey. The Furies
were repreſented with a grim and hideous
aſpect, with black and bloody garments, and
with ſerpents wreathing round their heads inſtead of hair: they held a burning torch in one
hand, and a whip of ſcorpions in the other,
and were always attended by terror, paleneſs,
rage, and death. In Hell they were ſeated
around the throne of Pluto, as the miniſters of
his vengeance.

NIGHT.

NIGHT.

Nox, or Night, one of the moſt ancient Deities among the Heathens, daughter of Chaos. From her union with her brother Erebus, by which is underſtood Darkneſs, or Hell itſelf, ſhe gave birth to the day and the light; ſhe was alſo called the mother of the Parcæ, Heſperides, Dreams, of Diſcord, Momus, Fraud, &c. She is called by ſome of the poëts the mother of all things, of Gods as well as of Men, and ſhe was worſhiped with great ſolemnity by the Ancients. She had a famous ſtatue in the temple of Diana, at Epheſus. It was uſual to offer her a black ſheep, as to the mother of the Furies. The cock was alſo offered to her, as that bird proclaims the approach of day during the darkneſs of the night. Nox is repreſented on a chariot, and covered with a veil beſpangled with ſtars. The conſtellations generally went before her as her conſtant meſſengers. Sometimes ſhe is ſeen holding two children in her arms; one of which is black, repreſenting death, and the other white,

repreſenting

reprefenting fleep.   Some of the moderns have
defcribed her as a woman veiled in mourning,
and crowned with poppies, in a chariot drawn
by owls and bats.

DEATH.

MORS, or Death, the daughter of night,
without a father. She was worfhiped by the
Ancients with great folemnity, yet fhe was not
regarded as an actual exifting power, but as an
imaginary being. Euripides introduces her in
one of his tragedies upon the ftage. The moderns reprefent her as a fkeleton, armed with a
fcythe and a fcymetar.

SLEEP.

SOMNUS, fon of Erebus and Nox, prefided over fleep.   His palace, according to
fome mythologifts, is a dark cave, where the
fun never penetrates. At the entrance is a
quantity

quantity of poppies and fomniferous herbs.
The God himfelf is reprefented as fleeping on
a bed of down, with black curtains. The
Dreams ftands around him, and Morpheus, his
principal minifter, watches to prevent the in-
trufion of any thing that might difturb his repofe. Morpheus is likewife fometimes himfelf
called the God of fleep; but he is more properly the God of dreams, and the attendant of
Somnus. Virgil makes mention of two gates
in the houfe of Sleep; one of clear ivory,
through which falfe dreams pafs; the other of
tranfparent horn, and through which true vi-
fions come to men.

JUDGES OF HELL.

MINOS.

MINOS, once king of Crete, son of Jupiter and Europa. He flourished about 1432 years before the Christian æra. He gave laws to his subjects, which still remained in full force in the age of the philosopher Plato, about a thousand years after the death of the legislator. his justice and moderation procured him the appellation of the favourite of the Gods, the confident of Jupiter, the wise legislator in every city of Greece; and, according to the poets, he was rewarded for his equity, after death, with the office of supreme and absolute judge in the Infernal Regions. In this capacity, he is represented sitting in the midst of the shades, and holding a sceptre in his hand. The dead plead their different causes before him, and the impartial judge shakes the fatal urn which contains the destinies of mankind. Minos married Ithona, by whom he had Lycastes, who was the father of Minos the second.

ÆACUS.

ÆACUS.

ÆACUS, the fon of Jupiter and Ægina, was king of the ifland of Œnopia, which he called by his mother's name. A peftilence having deftroyed all his fubjects, he entreated Jupiter to repeople his kingdom, and in compliance with his requeft, all the ants which were in an old oak, were changed into men, and called by Æacus, Myrmidons, which fignifies an ant. Æacus married Endeis, by whom he had Telemon and Peleus. He afterwards had Phocus by Pfamathe, one of the Nereids. He was a man of fuch integrity, that the Ancients have made him one of the judges of Hell, with Minos and Radamanthus.

RHADA-

RHADAMANTHUS.

RHADAMANTHUS, a son of Jupiter and Europa, and brother of Minos. He was born in Crete, which he abandoned when he was about thirty years old; he passed into some of the Cyclades, where he reigned with so much justice and impartiality, that the Ancients have said, he likewise became one of the judges of Hell, and that he was employed in the Infernal Regions, in obliging the dead to confess their crimes, and in punishing them for their offences. Rhadamanthus reigned not only over some of the Cyclades, but also over many of the Greek cities of Asia.

THE

THE MOST FAMOUS OF THE CONDEMNED IN HELL.

THE GIANTS.

THE Giants were fons of Cœlus and Terra: they were defcribed as men of uncommon fta- ture, with ftrength proportioned to their gi- gantic fize. Some of them, as Cottus, Bria- reus, and Gyges, had each fifty heads, and an hundred arms, and ferpents inftead of legs. Their afpect was terrible, their hair hung loofe about their fhoulders, and their beard was fuf- fered to grow unmolefted. Pallene, and its neigh- bourhood, was the place of their refidence. The defeat of the Titans, to whom they were nearly related, incenfed them againft Jupiter, and they all confpired to dethrone him. The God was alarmed, and called all the Deities to affift him againft a powerful enemy, who made ufe of rocks, oaks, and burning wood for their wea- pons, and who had already heaped Mount Offa upon Pelion, in order to fcale the walls of

Heaven.

Heaven. At the fight of fuch dreadful adverfaries, the Gods fled with the utmoft confternation into Egypt, where they affumed the form
of different animals, to fcreen themfelves from
their purfuers. Jupiter, however, remembered
that thefe enemies were not invincible, provided
he called a mortal to his affiftance ; and, by the
advice of Pallas, he armed his fon Hercules in
his caufe. With the aid of this celebrated hero,
the Giants were foon put to flight and defeated.
Some were crufhed to pieces under mountains,
or buried in the fea, and others were flead alive,
or beaten to death with clubs. Briareus, who
had hurled an hundred rocks againft Jupiter at
one throw, was bound with an hundred chains,
and thruft under Mount Ætna, where, as often
as he moves, the mountain cafts forth flames
and fmoke. To thefe Giants, fons of Coelus
and Terra, may be added Typhœus, or Typhon, fon of Tartarus and Terra, according to
fome, he was produced by Juno's ftriking the
earth; and Tityus, the fon of Jupiter and Elara,
the daughter of Orchomenos. Typhœus had
an hundred heads like thofe of a ferpent or a
dragon; flames of devouring fire darted from
his mouth and from his eyes, and he uttered horrid yells, like the diffonant fhrieks of
different animals. He was no fooner born,

than

than to avenge the death of his brothers, the
Giants, he made war againſt Heaven; but
the father of the Gods ſtruck him with
his thunder-bolts, and overthrew him, and,
leſt he ſhould riſe again, he laid the whole
iſland of Sicily upon him. The Egyptians called him Typhon. They looked upon
him to be the cauſe of all evil, and on that account generally repreſented him as a wolf or a
crocodile. Tityus attempted to offer violence
to Latona; but the Goddeſs delivered herſelf
from his importunities, by calling her children
to her aſſiſtance, who killed the Giant with their
arrows. He was afterwards placed in Hell,
where a vulture perpetually fed upon his en-
trails, which grew again as ſoon as devoured.
It is ſaid that Tityus covered nine acres when
ſtretched on the ground.

THE TITANS.

TO theſe may be added the Titans, the ſons
of Titan, who was the eldeſt of the children
of Cœlus. They are ſometimes reckoned
among the Giants, as they were likewiſe of a

L 3   gigantic

gigantic ftature, and with proportionable ftrength. The wars of the Titans againft the Gods, are much celebrated in mythology: they are often confounded with thofe of the Giants; but it is to be obferved, that the war of the Titans was againft Saturn, and that of the Giants againft Jupiter. The number both of the Giants and Titans feems to be very uncertain.

PHLEGYAS.

PHLEGYAS, a fon of Mars, King of the Lapithæ in Theffaly; he was the father of Ixion, and of Coronis, to whom Apollo offered violence. When the father heard that his daughter had been thus abufed, he marched againft Delphi, and reduced the temple of the God to afhes. This fo highly incenfed Apollo, that he put Phlegyas to death, and placed him in Hell, where a huge ftone hangs over his head, and keeps him in continual dread, by its appearance of being ready to fall, and crufh him every moment.

IXION.

IXION.

IXION, fon of Phlegyas, according to fome, but others make him fon of Leontes, or of Antion. He married Dia, daughter of Einoneus or Deioneus, and promifed his father-in-law a valuable prefent of horfes, for the choice he had made of him to be his daughter's hufband. His unwillingnefs, however, to fulfil his promife, or induced Deioneus to have recourfe to violence to obtain it, and he ftole away fome of his horfes. Ixion concealed his refentment under the mafk of friendfhip, and invited his father-in-law to a feaft, where he murdered him. This premeditated treachery fo irritated all the neighbouring Princes, that Ixion was univerfally fhunned and defpifed. Jupiter at length took compaffion on him, carried him to Heaven, and there placed him at the table of the Gods. Such a favour, which ought to have awakened the gratitude of Ixion, ferved only to make him forget himfelf. He became enamoured of Juno, and attempted to feduce her; but fhe having informed Jupiter of his infolence, the God made

a cloud

a cloud in the shape of Juno, and sent it to the place where Ixion expected to find the Goddess. The deceived lover embraced it, and to this adventure the Centaurs were said to owe their origin. Ixion was immediately after this banished from Heaven, and having had the impudent rashness to boast that he had seduced the wife of Jove, the God struck him with his thunder, and precipitated him into Hell, where he was fastened to a wheel, which continually whirls round.

SALMONEUS.

SALMONEUS, the son of Æolus and Enaretta, whom arried Alcidice, by whom he had Tyro. Salmoneus wished to be thought a God, and to receive divine honours from his subjects, he therefore imitated the thunder of Jupiter, by driving his chariot over a brazen bridge, which he had caused to be built over his city, and he darted burning torches on every side to imitate the lightning. Jupiter provoked at this impiety, struck Salmoneus with a thunder-bolt, and hurled him headlong into the Infernal Regions, where he was placed near his brother Sisyphus.

SISYPHUS.

SISYPHUS.

SISYPHUS, a brother of Salmoneus and Athamas, the moſt crafty Prince of the heroic ages. He married Merope, the daughter of Atlas, or, according to ſome, of Pandareus, by whom he had ſeveral children. He built Ephire, called afterwards Corinth. He ſeduced Tyro, the daughter of Salmoneus, becauſe he had been told by an oracle, that his children by his brother's daughter, would avenge ſome injuries which he had ſuffered from the malevolence of Salmoneus. Tyro, however, as Hygynus ſays, deſtroyed the two ſons whom ſhe had by her uncle. After his death, Siſyphus was condemned in Hell, to roll to the top of a hill a large ſtone, which had no ſooner reached the ſummit than it fell back into the plain with impetuoſity, and rendered his puniſhment eternal. The cauſes of this rigorous ſentence are variouſly reported. Some attribute it to his continual depredations in the neighbouring country, and his cruelty in laying heaps of ſtones upon the bodies of thoſe whom he had plundered, and ſuffering them to expire in the moſt agonizing

torments.

torments. Others, to the infult which he offered to Pluto, in chaining Death in his palace,
and detaining her till Mars, at the requeft of
the King of Hell, went to deliver her from her
confinement. Others fuppofe, that Jupiter in-
inflicted this punifhment upon him, becaufe he
told Afopus where his daughter Ægina had
been carried by her ravifher.

The more received opinion, however, is, that
Sifyphus, on his death-bed, entreated his wife
to leave his body unburied, and when he came
into the kingdom of Pluto, he obtained permiffion to return upon earth, to punifh this
feeming neglect of his wife, but, however, on
promife of immediately returning. He was no
fooner out of the Infernal Regions, than he violated his engagements; and when he was at laft
brought back to Hell by Mars, Pluto, to punifh
his want of fidelity and honour, condemned
him to roll a huge ftone to the top of a mountain, as has been faid.

TANTALUS.

TANTALUS.

TANTALUS, a King of Lydia, fon of Jupiter, by a nymph called Plota. He was father of Niobe, Pelops, &c. by Dione, one of the Atlantides, called by fome Euryanaffa. Tantalus is reprefented by the Poets, as punifhed in Hell, with an infatiable thirft, and placed up to the chin in the midft of a pool of water, which, however, flows away as foon as he attempts to tafte it. There hangs alfo above his head, a bough richly loaded with delicious fruit, which, as foon as he attempted to feize, is carried away from his reach by a fudden blaft of wind. According to fome mytholifts, his punifhment is to fit, like Phlegyas, under a huge ftone which is hung at fome diftance over his head; and as it feems every moment ready to fall, he is kept in perpetual terrors and never-ceafing apprehenfions of being crufhed by it. This eternal punifhment is faid to have been inflicted on Tantalus, for his cruelty and impiety in killing his fon Pelops, and in ferving him up as food before the Gods, whofe divinity and power he wifhed to prove, when they had

ftopped

stopped at his house in passing over Phrygia; others say, that it was because he stole away the nectar and ambrosia from the tables of the Gods, when he was admitted into the assemblies of Heaven, and gave it to mortals on earth.

THE DANAIDES.

THE Danaides were the fifty daughters of Danaus, King of Argos. When their uncle Ægyptus came from Egypt with his fifty sons, they were promised in marriage to their cousins, and before the celebration of the nuptials, Danaus, who had been informed by an oracle that he was to die by the hands of one of his sons-in-law, made his daughters solemnly promise, that they would destroy their husbands : They were provided with daggers by their father, and all, except Hypermnestra, stained their hands with the blood of their cousins the first night of their nuptials ; and as a pledge of their obedience to their fathers injunctions, they presented him with the heads of the murdered sons of Ægyp-.

tus

tus. Hypermneſtra was ſummoned to appear before her father, and anſwer for her diſobedience, in ſuffering her huſband Lynceus to eſcape ; but the unanimous voice of the people declared her innocent, and ſhe dedicated a temple to the Goddeſs of Perſuaſion. Some authors ſay, that the ſiſters were purified of this murder, by Mercury and Minerva, by order of Jupiter ; but according to the more received opinion, they were condemned to a ſevere puniſhment in Hell, and were compelled to fill with water a veſſel full of holes ; ſo that the water ran out as faſt as poured into it, and therefore their labour was infinite, and their puniſhment eternal. The Denaides were alſo called Belides, from their grandfather Belus.

MONSTERS,

MONSTERS OF HELL.

THE CENTAURS.

THERE are many strange pictures of these infernal monsters, among which are the Centaurs, who were the ancient inhabitants of Thessalia, and the first who tamed horses, and made use of them in war. Their neighbours, who first saw them on horseback, thought that they had partly the members of a man, aud partly the limbs of an horse; but the Poets say, that they were produced from the cloud which Ixion mistook for Juno, and that they were monsters, half man and half horse. Bacchus is said by some to have overcame them; but according to others, they were extirpated by Hercules, when he was going to hunt the boar of Erymanthus.

GERYON.

GERYON.

GERYON was a famous monster, born from the union of Chryfaor with Callirkoe. He is reprefented by the Poets as having three bodies, and three heads. He lived in the Ifland of Gades, where he kept numerous flocks, which were guarded by a two-headed dog, called Orthos, and by Eurythion. Hercules, by order of Euryftheus, went to Gades and deftroyed Geryon, Orthos, and Eurythion, and carried away all the flocks and herds to Tirynthus.

THE HARPYES.

THE Harpyes were fo called from their rapacity. They were winged monfters which had the faces of women, the bodies of vultures, and had their feet and fingers armed with fharp
claws,

claws. They were three in number, Aello, Ocypete, and Celeno, daughters of Neptune and Terra. They were sent by Juno to plunder the tables of Phineus; whence they were driven to the islands called Strophades, by Zethes and Calais. They emitted an infectious smell, and spoiled whatever they touched by their filth and excrements. They made war against Æneas during his voyage towards Italy, and predicted many of the calamites which attended him.

THE GORGONS.

THE Gorgons were three celebrated sisters, daughters of Phorcys and Ceto. Their names were Stheno, Euryale, and Medusa. They were all immortal, except Medusa. According to the Mythologists, their hairs were entwined with serpents, their hands were brass, their bodies were covered with impenetrable scales, their teeth were as long as the tusks of a wild boar, and they turned to stones all those on whom they fixed their regards. According to

Ovid

Ovid, however, Medufa alone had fnakes in her hair, and he fays that this was occafioned by the refentment of Minerva, in whofe temple Medufa had gratified the paffion of Neptune, who was enamoured of her on account of the beautiful colour of her hair, which the Goddefs changed into ferpents. Æfchylus fays, that thefe three fifters had only one tooth and one eye between them, of which they had the ufe each in her turn; and he afferts, that it was at the time they were exchanging the eye, that Perfeus attacked them, and cut off Medufa's head. According to fome authors, Perfeus, when he went to the conqueft of the Gorgons, was armed with an inftrument like a fcythe by Mercury, and provided with a looking-glafs by Minerva; befides winged fhoes, and the helmet of Pluto, which rendered the wearer invifible. With thefe weapons, Perfeus obtained an eafy victory; after which he reftored his arms to the different Deities whofe favour and affiftance he had fo happily experienced. The head of Medufa remained in his hands, and after he had finifhed all his laborious expeditions, he prefented it to Minerva, who placed it on her Ægis, with which fhe turned to ftones all fuch as fixed their eyes upon it. It was faid, that after the conqueft of the

Gorgons,

Gorgons, Perseus took his flight in the air towards Æthiopia; and that the drops of blood
which fell to the ground from Medusa's head,
produced all those serpents which have ever
since infested the sandy deserts of Lybia. The
horse Pegasus also was said to arise from the
blood of the Gorgon, as well as Chrysaor, with
his golden sword. The residence of the Gorgons was beyond the ocean, towards the West,
according to Hesiod. Æschylus makes them
inhabit the Eastern parts of Scythia; and Ovid,
as the more received opinion, maintains, that
they dwelt in the inland parts of Lybia, near
the lake of Triton, or the gardens of the Hesperides. Diodorus, and others, explain the
fable of the Gorgons, by supposing that they
were a warlike race of women near the Amazons, whom Perseus, with the help of a large
army, totally destroyed.

THE CHIMÆRA.

THE Chimæra, a celebrated monster, sprung
from Echidna and Typhon: it had three heads,
that

that of a lion, a goat, and a dragon, and continually vomited flames : the foreparts of its body were thofe of a lion, the middle like thofe of a goat, and the hinder parts were thofe of a dragon. It ufually inhabited Lycia, about the reign of Jobates ; by whofe orders Bellerophon, mounted on the horfe Pegafus, is faid to have overcome it. This fabulous tradition is explained by the recollection that there was a burning mountain in Lycia, whofe top was the refort of lions, on account of its defolate wildernefs. The middle which was fruitful, was covered with goats ; and, at the bottom, the marfhy ground abounded with ferpents. Bellerophon is faid to have conquered the Chimæra, becaufe he firft made his habitation on that mountain. Plutarch fays, that it was the captain of fome pirates, who adorned their fhips with the images of a lion, a goat, and a dragon.

THE

THE SPHINX.

THE Sphinx a monſter, which had the head and boſom of a woman, the body of a dog, the tail of a ſerpent, the wings of a bird, the paws of a lion, and a human voice. It ſprang from the union of Othos with the Chimæra, or of Typhon with Echidna. The Sphinx had been ſent into the neighbourhood of Thebes by Juno, in order to puniſh the family of Cadmus, which ſhe perſecuted with immortal hatred, and it kept all that part of Bœotia under continual alarms, by propoſing enigmas, and devouring the inhabitants who were unable to explain them. In the midſt of their conſternation, the Thebans were told by the oracle, that the Sphinx would deſtroy herſelf, as ſoon as the enigma which ſhe then propoſed was explained. She demanded, What animal walked on four legs in the morning, on two at noon, and on three in the evening? Upon this Creon, King of Thebes, promiſed his crown, and his ſiſter Jocaſta in marriage, to him who could deliver his country from the monſter, by a ſucceſsful

explanation

explanation of her enigma. It was at laft happily explained by Œdipus, who obferved, that
this animal was man, who walked on his hands
and feet in his infancy, the morning of his life;
at the noon of life he walked erect on two legs,
and in the evening of his days, he fupported his
infirmities upon a ftaff. The Sphinx no fooner
heard this folution, than fhe dafhed her head
againft a rock, and inftantly expired. Some
mythologifts endeavour to unriddle the fabulous
traditions concerning the Sphinx, by the fuppofition, that one of the daughters of Cadmus,
or of Laius, infefted the country of Thebes by
her continual depredations, becaufe fhe had
been refufed a part of her father's poffeffions.
The lions paw expreffed, as they obferve, her
cruelty. The body of the dog her lafciviouf-
nefs. Her enigmas, the fnares which fhe laid
for ftrangers and travellers ; and her wings the
difpatch which fhe ufed in her expeditions.

Having mentioned Œdipus, his ftory is too
remarkable to be omitted. He was a fon of
Laius, King of Thebes, by Jocafta, becaufe
defcended from Venus by his father's fide :.
Œdipus was born to be expofed to all the dangers and calamities which Juno could inflict:
Laius had been warned by an oracle, that he
                                                    muft

muſt periſh by the hands of his own ſon ; and, therefore, when Œdipus was born, Jocaſta was commanded by her huſband to deſtroy him immediately, but ſhe, unable to obey, gave the child to one of her domeſtics, with orders to expoſe him on the mountains. This man bored the feet of the infant, and ſuſpended him with a twig, by the heels, to a tree on Mount Cithæron, where he was ſoon found by one of the ſhepherds of Polybus, King of Corinth, who carried him to Peribæa, the wife of Polybus. He was kindly received by her ; and as ſhe had no children, ſhe educated him as her own ſon, and named him Œdipus, from the ſwelling of his feet. He ſoon became, on account of his extraordinary accompliſhments, the admiration of the age. His companions envied his ſuperior ſtrength and addreſs ; and one of them, to mortify his riſing ambition, told him that his birth was illigitimate. This raiſed his doubts, and he applied to the Queen to reſolve them, who tenderly anſwered, that his ſuſpicions were ill-founded. Œdipus, however, was not ſatisfied, and he went to conſult the oracle at Delphi. He was then warned not to return to his country, and told, that if he did ſo, he muſt neceſſarily become the murderer of his father, and the huſband of his mother. Filled with

horror

horror at this answer of the oracle, and looking
upon Corinth as his country, he resolved never
to return thither, where such calamities ap-
parently awaited him. He travelled towards
Phocis, and, in his journey, met in a narrow
road, a majestic stranger, on a chariot, who
haughtily ordered Œdipus to make way for
him. Œdipus refused, and a contest ensued,
in which the stranger was killed, and this
stranger was Laius. The unhappy son, ignorant of the name and quality of the man whom
he had slain, pursued his journey, and was at-
tracted to Thebes, by the fame of the Sphinx.
He overcame her, married his mother, and thus
innocently, though fatally, accomplished the
dreadful oracle. He had by Jocasta two sons,
Eteocles and Polynices, and two daughters,
Ismene and Antigone. Some years after, the
Theban territories were visited with a plague,
and the oracle declared, that it should cease
only, when the murderer of Laius was banished from Bœotia. As the death of Laius
had never been examined into, and the circum-
stances that attended it, never known, this answer of the oracle gave the greatest concern to
the Thebans; but Œdipus, the friend of his
people, resolved to overcome every difficulty by
the strictest enquiries. His researches proved but
too

too fuccefsful for his peace, and he foon found that he himfelf was the murderer of Laius, and that Laius was his father. This dreadful difcoverey, joined to that of his having committed inceft with his mother, plunged Œdipus into a ftate of fuch defperation, that he put out his own eyes as unworthy to fee the light, and banifhed himfelf from Thebes, or as fome fay, he was banifhed by his own fons. He retired towards Attica, led by his daughter Antigone. He approached Colonos, where there was a grove facred to the Furies. Here he remembered that he was doomed by the Oracle, to die in fuch a place, and to become the fource of profperity to the country where his bones fhould be interred. A meffenger was fent to Thefeus, King of that country, to inform him of the refolution of Œdipus. When Thefeus arrived, Œdipus, with a prophetic voice, declared to him, that the Gods had called him to die in that place, and to convince him of the truth of this affertion, he walked himfelf without a guide, to the fpot where he was fated to expire, when immediately the earth opened, and Œdipus difappeared. Some fuppofe that Œdipus had no children by Jocafta, and that fhe murdered herfelf as foon as fhe knew the inceft which fhe had committed. According to thefe writers,

writers, the four children of Œdipus, were by
Euriganea, the daughter of Periphas, whom he
was said to marry after the death of Jocasta.
His tomb was near the Areopagus, in the
age of Paufanias. After the voluntary ba-
niſhment of Œdipus, his two ſons, Eteocles and Polynices, ageeed that they would
both ſhare the royalty, and reign alternately,
each a year. Eteocles by right of ſeniority, firſt
afcended the throne ; but after the firſt year of
his reign was expired, he refuſed to yield the
crown to his brother, according to their mutual
agreement. Polynices therefore refolved to
puniſh ſuch an open violation of a ſolemn engagement, implored the aſſiſtance of Adraſtus,
king of Argos, who gave him his daughter in
marriage, and ſupplied him with a powerful
army, headed by ſeven famous generals : Eteocles on his part did not remain inactive ; he
choſe ſeven brave chiefs to oppoſe the ſeven
leaders of the Argives, and ſtationed them at
the ſeven gates of the city. Much blood had
been ſhed in ſlight and unavailing ſkirmiſhes ;
when it was at length agreed between the two
brothers, that the war ſhould be decided by them
in ſingle combat. They both fell in an engagement conducted with the moſt inveterate
fury on either ſide ; and it is even ſaid, that the

aſhes

M

aſhes of theſe two brothers, who had been ſo inimical to each other, ſeparated themſelves on the funeral pile which had been raiſed for them in common, and that two diſtinct flames were ſeen to aſcend from it, as if to prove that they were ſtill ſenſible to reſentment, and hoſtile to reconciliation. The two daughters of Œdipus, Antigone and Iſmena, both periſhed by the cruelty of their uncle Creon, who had again ſucceeded to the throne of Thebes, after the death of Eteocles and Polynices. The death of Antigone is the ſubject of one of the tragedies of Sophocles.

CHARON.

CHARON.

A SON of Erebus and Nox. He conducted the fouls of the dead, in a boat over the rivers Styx and Acheron, to the Infernal Regions. Such as had not been honoured with a funeral were not permitted to enter his bark, till they had wandered on the fhore for one hundred years. If any living perfon prefented himfelf to crofs the Stygian Lake, he could not be admitted; unlefs he could fhow Charon a golden bough, which could only be obtained from the Sibyl who was a Prophetefs of Apollo; and Charon was imprifoned a year becaufe he had ferried over (though againft his will) Hercules, without this paffport. Charon is reprefented as a robuft old man, with a hideous countenance, ong white beard, and piercing eyes. His garment is ragged and filthy, and his forehead is covered with wrinkles. As all the dead were fuppofed to pay a piece of money to this grim ferryman; it was ufual among the Ancients to place a piece of money under the tongue of the deceafed for Charon. This fable of Charon and his bark feems to be borrowed

from

from the Egyptians; who had a cuſtom of carrying their dead acroſs a lake, to a place where
ſentence was paſſed over them, and, according to
their good or bad actions, they were honoured
with a ſplendid burial, or left unnoticed in the
open air.

CERBERUS.

A DOG of Pluto, called the Porter of Hell, the offspring of Typhon and Echidna. He had fifty heads according to Hesiod, and three according to other Mythologists, He was stationed at the entrance of Hell, as a watchful keeper, to prevent the living from entering the Infernal Regions, and the dead from escaping from their confinement. It was usual for those heroes who during their lifetime visited the kingdom of Pluto, to appease the barking mouths of Cerberus with a cake, but Orpheus lulled him to sleep with his lyre, and Hercules dragged him from Hell when he went to redeem Alceste.

RIVERS OF HELL.

ACHERON.

ACHERON was a fon of Ceres, without a father. He concealed himfelf in Hell for fear of the Titans, and was changed into a bitter ftream, over which the fouls of the dead are firft conveyed. It receives departed fouls, becaufe a dead languor feizes them at the hour of diffolution. Some make Acheron a fon of Titan, and fuppofe that he was plunged into Hell by Jupiter, for fupplying the Titans with water. Acheron is often taken for Hell itfelf.

STYX.

STYX.

THE moft celebrated river of Hell, round which it flows nine times. According to fome writers, the Styx was a fmall river of Nonacris in Arcadia, whofe waters were fo cold and poifonous, that they proved fatal to all thofe who tafted them: they even confumed iron, and broke all veffels. The wonderful properties of this water, fuggefted the idea that it was a river of Hell; efpecially as it difappeared in the earth, a little below its fountain head. The Gods held the waters of Styx in fuch veneration, that they always fwore by them, an oath which was inviolable. If any of the Gods had perjured themfelves, Jupiter obliged them to drink the waters of the Styx, which lulled them for one whole year in a ftate of infenfibility; for the nine following years they were deprived of the ambrofia and nectar of the Gods; and after the expiration of the term of their penance, they were re-admitted into the affembly of the Deities, and reftored to all their former privileges. It is faid that this veneration was paid to the Styx, becaufe it received its name from the Nymph Styx, who with her three daughters affifted Jupiter in his war againft the Titans.

COCYTUS.

COCYTUS.

THE unwholefomenefs of its waters, and its vicinity to the Acheron, have given occafion to the poets, to call it one of the rivers of Hell.

PHLEGETHON,

WHICH fwells with waves of fire, and all its ftreams are flames.

LETHE.

LETHE,

OR the River of Oblivion; whose waters the dead were said to drink after they had been confined for a certain space in Tartarus. It had the power of making them forget whatever they had done, seen, or heard before their drinking it. There is a river of Africa called Lethe, near the Syrtes, which flows under the ground, and some time after rises again; whence it is thought originates the fable of the Lethean Stream of oblivion.

TARTARUS,

—

ONE of the regions of Hell, where, according to the Ancients, the most impious and guilty among mankind were punished. It was surrounded with a brazen wall, and its entrance was continually hidden from the sight by a cloud of darkness, which is represented as three times more gloomy than the obscurest night. According to Hesiod, it was a separate prison, at a greater distance from the earth than the earth is from the heavens. Virgil says that it was surrounded by three impenetrable walls, and by the impetuous and burning streams of the river Phlegethon. The entrance was by a large and lofty tower, whose gates were supported by columns of adamant, which neither Gods nor men could open. Here were punished such as had been disobedient to their parents, traitors, adulterers, faithless ministers, and such as had undertaken unjust and cruel wars, or had betrayed their friends for interest. It was also the place where Ixion, Tityus, the Danaides, Tantalus, Sisyphus, &c. were tormented, according to Ovid.

ELYSIUM,

ELYSIUM,

OR the Elyſian Fields, a place or iſland in
the Infernal Regions, where, according to the
mythology of the Ancients, the ſouls of the virtuous were placed after death. Their happineſs was ſuppoſed to be complete, their pleaſures innocent and refined. Bowers for ever
green, delightful meadows, with pleaſant
ſtreams, were the moſt ſtriking objects. The
air pure, ſerene, and temperate: the birds continually warbling in the groves. Another ſun
and other ſtars gave light to theſe bleſt abodes.
The employments of the inhabitants were various. The manes of Achilles are deſcribed
as waging war with the wild-beaſts, while the
Trojan chiefs are innocently exerciſing themſelves in managing horſes, or in handling arms.
To theſe amuſements ſome poets have added
continual feaſting and revelry; and they pretend, that the Elyſian Fields were filled with
all the incontinence and voluptuouſneſs which
could gratify the deſires of the ſenſual. The

M 6 Elyſium

Elyſium was, according to ſome, in the For-
tunate iſlands on the coaſts of Africa, in the
Atlantic ; others place it in the iſland of Leuce.
According to the authority of Virgil, it was ſi-
tuate in Italy, and according to Lucian, it
was near the moon, or if we believe Plutarch,
in the centre of the earth.

DEMI GODS AND HEROES.

ÆSCULAPIUS	ULYSSES
HERCULES	ACHILLES
JASON	ÆNEAS
THESEUS	CADMUS.
PERSEUS	

CASTOR AND POLLUX.

ORPHEUS AND AMPHION.

ÆSCULAPIUS.

—

ÆSCULAPIUS was called the God of Medicine, yet he was mortal. As he was the friend of mankind, he feems to claim a place among thofe who were ftiled the patrons and prefervers of them. He was the fon of Apollo and Coronis. The God, in a fit of Jealoufy, deftroyed his miftrefs with his arrows; but preferved the infant, and entrufted his education to Chiron the Centaur, who taught him the art of medicine. Some authors fay, that Coronis fled from her father, to avoid the difcovery of her pregnancy, and that fhe expófed her child near Epidaurus. A goat of the flocks of Arefthanas, gave him her milk, and the dog which kept the flock, ftood by to fhelter him from injury. He was found by Arefthanas, who went in fearch of his ftray goat, and who faw his head furounded with refplendent rays of light. Æfculapius was Phyfician to the Argonauts. He faved the lives of fo many by his art, that Pluto complained of it to Jupiter, who ftruck Æfculapius with thunder. He received divine

honours

honours after his death, chiefly at Epidaurus, Pergamus, Athens, Smyrna, &c. Goats, bulls, lambs, and pigs were facrificed to him, and the cock and the ferpent were facred to him. Rome having been delivered from a plague, built a temple to the God of Medicine; who, as was fuppofed, had come thither in the form of a ferpent, and hid himfelf among the reeds, in an ifland of the Tyber. Æfculapius is reprefented with a large beard, holding in his hand a ftaff, round which wreathed a ferpent. His other hand is fometimes fupported on the head of a ferpent. This reptile is more particularly facred to him, becaufe the antient Phyficians ufed it in their prefcriptions. He had married Epione, by whom he had two fons, famous for their fkill in medicine; Machaon, and Podalirus; and four daughters, of whom Hygiea, the Goddefs of Health, is moft known. Some have fuppofed that Æfculapius lived a fhort time after the Trojan war.

Cicero fays there were three of this name; the firft a fon of Apollo, worfhiped in Arcadia; the fecond, a brother of Mercury; and the third a man who firft taught medicine.

HERCULES.

HERCULES.

HERCULES was the moft celebrated of all the heroes of antiquity, and after his death was ranked among the Gods, and received divine honours. According to the Ancients, there were many perfons of the fame name. Diodorus mentions three, Cicero fix, and fome authors extend the number to no lefs than forty-three. Of all thefe, the fon of Jupiter and Alcmena, generally called the Theban, is the moft known; and to him, as may eafily be imagined, the actions of the others have been attributed. The birth of Hercules is thus related; Electryon, King of Mycenæ, had promifed his crown and his daughter Alcmena to him who could revenge the death of his fons, who were all killed in a battle by the Teleboans, a people of Ætolia. Amphitrion, a Theban Prince, offered himfelf, and was accepted, on condition that he fhould not approach Alcmena till he had obtained a complete victory. Jupiter, in the mean time, who was captivated with the charms of Alcmena, taking

advantage

advantage of the abfence of Amphitrion on this expedition, affumed his form and features, and introduced himfelf to the daughter of Electryon, as her hufband returned victorious. Soon after Amphitrion himfelf, having fulfilled his engagements, returned, and learned the deception which had been practifed upon his wife; but being convinced of the purity of her intentions, and perhaps proud of the dignity of his rival, he teftified no refentment on the occafion. Alcmena became pregnant of Hercules, by Jupiter, and of Iphiclus, by Amphitrion. When fhe was near her term, Jupiter having boafted in Heaven that a child would be born to him that day, to whom he would give abfolute power over his neighbours, and even all the children of his own blood. Juno, who was jealous of her hufband's amour with Alcmena, made him fwear by the Styx, and then exerted her power to prolong the travails of Alcmena, haftening, at the fame time, the bringing forth of the wife of Sthenelus, king of Argos, who, at the term of feven months, had a fon called Euryftheus; Hercules was therefore fubjected to the power of Euryftheus. The young hero was brought up at Tirynthus; or, according to Diodorus, at Thebes; and before he had completed his eighth month, the jealoufy of

Juno,

Juno, intent upon his deſtruction, ſent two ſnakes to devour him; but the child, unterrified at the ſight of the ſerpents, boldly ſeized them in both his hands, and ſqueezed them to death, while his brother Iphiclus alarmed the houſe with his ſhrieks. Hercules was early inſtructed in the liberal arts, and Caſtor, the ſon of Tindarus, taught him the manly exerciſes; of Erytus, he learned the uſe of the bow; and of Autolychus, how to drive a chariot; of Linus, how to play upon the lyre; and of Eumolpus, to ſing. He, like the reſt of his illuſtrious contemporaries, ſoon after became a pupil of the Centaur, Chiron, and under him, he perfected, and rendered himſelf the moſt valiant and accompliſhed perſon of the age. In his eighteenth year, he reſolved to deliver the neighbourhood of Mount Cithæron, from a huge lion, which preyed on the flocks of Amphitrion, his ſuppoſed father, and which laid waſte the adjacent country. He went to the court of Theſpius, king of Theſpis, who ſhared in the general calamity. He was there well received, and entertained during fifty days, in which time he is ſaid to have gained the love of the fifty daughters of the king. After he had deſtroyed the lion of Mount Cithæron, he delivered his country from the annual tribute of an hundred oxen, which

which is paid to Erginus ; and afterwards killed
Erginus himfelf, who had invaded Bœotia, to
avenge the death of his fervants who had been
flain by Hercules, when they were fent to demand the tribute. Such public fervices rendered the young hero the object of univerfal admiration ; and Creon, who then fat on the
throne of Thebes, rewarded his patriotic deeds,
by giving him his daughter Megara in marriage, and entrufting him with the government
of his kingdom. But Euryftheus, informed of
his fucceffes and rifing greatnefs, now fum-
moned him to appear at Mycenæ, and perform
the labours which, by priority of birth, he was
empowered to impofe upon him. Hercules refufed to comply, and Juno, to punifh his dif-
obedience, rendered him fo delirious, that he
killed his own children by Megara, fuppofing
them to be the offspring of Euryftheus. When
he recovered the ufe of his reafon, he was fo
ftruck with the misfortune, which had been the
effect of his infanity, that he concealed himfelf,
and retired from the fociety of men for fome
time. He afterwards confulted the Oracle of
Apollo, and was told, that he muft be fubfervient, during twelve years, to the will of Euryftheus, in compliance to the decree of Jupiter ; and that, after he had atchieved the moft

famous

famous exploits, he ſhould be reckoned among
the Gods. So plain and deciſive an anſwer,
determined Hercules to go to Mycenæ, and to
ſubmit with fortitude, to whatever Gods or
men might impoſe upon him. Euryſtheus,
ſeeing ſo great a man totally ſubjected to him,
and apprehenſive of ſo powerful an enemy, commanded him to atchieve a number of enter-
prizes, the moſt difficult and arduous ever
known, generally called the twelve labours of
Hercules. He was by the favour of the Gods,
completely armed when he undertook his labours. He had received a coat of arms from
Minerva, together with a helmet, a ſword from
Mercury, a horſe from Neptune, a ſhield from
Jupiter, a bow and arrows from Apollo, and
from Vulcan a golden cuiraſs and brazen buſ-
kins, with a celebrated club of braſs. The firſt
labour impoſed upon Hercules, by Euryſtheus,
was to kill the lion of Nemæ, which ravaged
the country near Mycenæ. The hero, unable
to deſtroy him with his arrows, boldly attacked
him with his club, purſued him to his den, and
after a cloſe and ſharp engagement, he choaked
him to death. He carried the dead beaſt on his
ſhoulders to Mycenæ, and ever after cloathed
himſelf with his ſkin. Euryſtheus was ſo aſtoniſhed at the ſight of the beaſt, and at the
courage

courage of Hercules, that he ordered him never
to enter the gates of the city when he returned
from his expeditions, but to attend his orders
without the walls. He even caused a brazen
veſſel to be made, into which he retired, whenever Hercules returned to Mycenæ. The ſecond labour of Hercules, was to deſtroy the
Lernæan Hydra, which had ſeven heads, according to Apollodorus; fifty according to Simo-
nides; and an hundred according to Diodorus.
This celebrated monſter he attacked with his
arrows, and ſoon after he came to a cloſe engagement, he deſtroyed, by means of his club,
the heads of his enemy; but this was produc-
tive of no advantage, for as ſoon as one head
was cruſhed to pieces, immediately two others
ſprung up, and the labour of Hercules would
have remained unfiniſhed, had not his friend
Iolaus burnt inſtantly, with a hot iron, the root
of the heads which he had cruſhed. This ſucceeded, and Hercules became victorious. He
afterwards opened the belly of the monſter, and
dipped his arrows in the gall, to render the
wounds which he made fatal and incurable.
He was ordered, in his third labour, to bring
alive and unhurt, into the preſence of Euryſtheus,
a ſtag famous for its incredible ſwiftneſs, its
golden horns and brazen feet. This celebrated
animal

animal frequented the neighbourhood of Œnoe,
and Hercules was employed a whole year in
continually pursuing it; at last he caught it
in a trap, or when tired with running, or, according to others, by slightly wounding it,
which slackened its speed; but, as he returned
victorious, he was met by Diana, who snatched
the stag from him, and severely reprimanded
him for molesting an animal which was sacred
to her. Hercules pleaded necessity, and by
representing the commands of Eurystheus, he
appeased the Goddess, and obtained the beast a
second time. The fourth labour, was to bring
alive to Eurystheus, a wild boar which ravaged
the neighbourhood of Erymanthus. In this expe-
pedition, Hercules destroyed the Centaurs, who
had violently attacked him, while he was con-
fiding in their hospitality. He caught the boar,
by closely pursuing him through the deep
snow. Eurystheus was so frightened at the
sight of the boar, that he hid himself in his
brazen vessel during several days. In his fifth
labour, Hercules was ordered to cleanse the
stables of Augias, where three thousand oxen
had been confined many years. The hero
changed the course of the river Alpheus, or,
according to some, of the Peneus, which immediately carried away all the filth from the stables.

For

For his fixth labour, he was commanded to kill the carnivorous birds which infefted the country near the lake Stymphalis, in Arcadia, and he deftroyed them by the affiftance of Minerva. In his feventh labour, he brought alive into Peloponnefus, a prodigious wild bull, which laid wafte the ifland of Crete. In his eighth labour, he was employed in obtaining the mares of Diomedes, which fed upon human flefh. —He killed Diomedes, and gave him to be eaten by his own mares, which he brought to Euryftheus: they were fent to Mount Olympus by the king of Mycenæ, where they were devoured by the wild beafts, or, according to fome, they were confecrated to Jupiter, and their breed ftill exifted in the age of Alexander the Great. For his ninth labour, he was obliged to obtain the girdle of Hippolite, queen of the Amazons. Hercules conquered her, took away her girdle, and afterwards gave her in marriage to Thefeus. In his tenth labour, he flew the monfter Geryon, king of Gades, and brought to Argos his numerous flocks, which fed upon human flefh. The eleventh labour, was to obtain apples from the garden of the Hefperides. The Hefperides were three Nymphs, daughters of Hefperus: they were appointed to guard the golden apples which

Juno

Juno prefented to Jupiter on the day of their
nuptials, and the place of their refidence, fixed
beyond the ocean by Hefiod, is more univerfally
believed to be near Mount Atlas, in Africa,
according to Apollodorus.   This celebrated
garden abounded with all kinds of delicious
fruits, which were carefully guarded by a dreadful dragon, which never flept.   Hercules, when
ordered to procure fome of the golden apples of
the Hefperides, was ignorant of the fituation
of the place where they were to be found, and
he applied to the Nymphs of the Po for information: they told him, that Nereus, if ma-
naged with addrefs, would direct him in his
purfuits.   Accordingly he feized the Sea-God
as he was afleep, who, unable to efcape from
his grafp, anfwered all the queftions which he
propofed.   Some fay, that Atlas procured the
apples for Hercules, while others maintain the
hero gathered them himfelf, and that he pre-
vioufly killed the watchful dragon which kept
the tree.   Thefe apples were brought to Euryftheus, and afterwards carried back by Minerva into the garden of the Hefperides, as they
could not be preferved in any other place.
The twelfth and laft, and the moft arduous of
the labours of Hercules, was to bring upon
earth the three-headed dog, Cerberus.   The
hero

OF THE HEATHEN DEITIES.

hero defcended into Hell by a cave on Mount
Tænarus. He was permitted by Pluto to
carry away his friends Thefeus and Pirithous,
who had been condemned to punifhment in the
Infernal Regions, and Cerberus was alfo granted
to his prayers, provided he made no ufe of arms,
but his own ftrength only to drag him away.
Hercules, as fome report, carried him back to
Hell, after he had brought him before Euryftheus. Befides all thefe labours, which the
jealoufy of Euryftheus impofed upon him, Hercules alfo atchieved others of his own accord,
equally great and celebrated. He killed the
robber Cacus, fon of Vulcan and Medufa, who
is alfo defcribed as a three-headed monfter, vomiting flames. He refided in Italy, and the
avenues of his cave were covered with human
bones. He plundered the neighbouring country; and when Hercules returned from the conqueft of Geryon, Cacus ftole fome of his oxen,
and dragged them backwards into his cave,
to prevent difcovery. The hero did not per-
ceive the theft till the lowing of his oxen,
being anfwered by the cows in the cave of Cacus,
he became acquainted with the lofs he had
fuftained. He haftened to the place, attacked
Cacus, feized, and ftrangled him in his arms,
though vomiting fire and fmoke. The giant,

N   Antæus,

Antæus, a son of Neptune and Terra, was deftroyed in like manner by Hercules. He was fo ftrong in wreftling, that he boafted he would erect a temple to his father with the fkulls of his conquered antagonifts. Hercules attacked him; and as he always received new ftrength from his mother, as often as he touched the earth, the hero lifted him up in the air, and preffed him to death in his arms. Eryx, a son of Butes and Venus, relying upon his great ftrength, challenged all ftrangers to fight with him in the combat of the Ceftus. Hercules accepted his challenge, after many had yielded to his fuperior force and dexterity, and Eryx was flain in the contention. Bufiris, a King of Egypt, fon of Neptune and Libya, facrificed all foreigners to Jupiter, with the moft favage cruelty. When Hercules vifited Egypt, Bufiris led him to the altar, bound hand and foot. The hero foon difengaged himfelf, and facrificed the tyrant, and the minifters of his cruelty, on the fame altar. Hercules accompanied the Argonauts to Colchis, before he delivered himfelf up to the King of Mycenæ. He affifted the Gods in their wars againft the Giants, and it was through him that Jupiter obtained a victory. He conquered Laomedon, and pillaged Troy; the walls of which city had been built

by

by Apollo and Neptune, whom Jupiter had banifhed from Heaven, and condemned to be fubfervient to the will of Laomedon for one year.
When the walls were finifhed, Laomedon refufed to reward the labours of the Gods, and
foon after his territories were laid wafte by the
fea, or Neptune, and his fubjects were vifited
by a peftilence fent by Apollo. Sacrifices were
offered to the offended Deities, but the calamities of the Trojans ftill encreafed ; and nothing
could appeafe the Gods, according to the words
of the Oracle, but annually to expofe to a fea-
monfter, a Trojan virgin. Whenever the
monfter appeared, the marriageable maidens
were affembled, and the lot decided which of
them was doomed to death for the good of her
country. When this calamity had continued
during feveral years, the lot fell upon Hefione,
daughter of Laomedon. The king was unwilling to part with his child, whom he loved
with uncommon tendernefs, but his refufal
would irritate more ftrongly the wrath of the
Gods. In the midft of this dread and hefita-
tion, Hercules came, and offered to deliver the
Trojans from this public affliction, if the king
would reward him with a certain number of
fine horfes. Laomedon promifed what he required ; but when the monfter was deftroyed,

he

he refufed to fufil his engagements, and Hercules was obliged to befiege Troy, and take it by force of arms. Laomedon was put to death, after a reign of 29 years. His daughter Hefione was given in marriage to Telamon, one of the heroes who had accompanied Hercules in this expedition; and Podarces, fon of Laomedon, who was afterwards fo well known by the name of Priam, was ranfomed by the Trojans, and placed upon his father's throne. When Iole, the daughter of Eurytus, king of Œchalia, of whom Hercules was deeply enamoured, was refufed to his entreaties, he fell into a fecond fit of infanity, and he murdered Iphitus, the only one of the fons of Eurytus, who had favoured his addreffes to Iole. He was fome time after purified of this murder, and his infanity ceafed; but the Gods ftill perfecuted him, and he was vifited by a diforder, which obliged him to apply to the Oracle of Delphi for relief. The coldnefs with which he was received by the Pythia, irritated him, and he refolved to plunder the Temple of Apollo, and carry away the facred tripod. The God oppofed it, and a fevere conflict was begun; the effects of which, nothing but the interference of Jupiter could have prevented. Hercules was afterwards told by the Oracle, that he muft be fold as a flave, and remain three

years

years in the moſt abjeѐt ſtate, before he could recover from his diſorder. He complied, and Mercury, by order of Jupiter, conducted him to Omphale, queen of Lydia, to whom he was ſold as a ſlave. Here he cleared all the country from robbers. Omphale, who was aſtoniſhed at his exploits, reſtored him to liberty, and married him. Hercules had Agelaus, or Lamon according to others, by Omphale, from whom Crœſus, king of Lydia, was deſcended. He became alſo enamoured of one of Omphale's female attendants, by whom he had Alcęus. After he had completed the years of his ſlavery, he returned to Peloponneſus, where he re-eſtabliſhed on the throne of Sparta, Tyndarus, who had been expelled by Hippocoon. He became one of the ſuitors of Dejanira, the daughter of Œneus, king Ætolia, and married her, after he had overcome all his rivals; among whom was Achelous, the ſon of Oceanus and Terra, or Tethys, God of the river of the ſame name in Epirus. Finding himſelf inferior in ſtrength to Hercules, he changed himſelf into a ſerpent, and afterwards into an ox. Hercules broke off one of his horns, and Achelous being defeated, retired into his bed of waters. Hercules was obliged to leave Calydon, his father-in-law's kingdom, becauſe he had inad-

N 3 vertently

vertently killed a man with a blow of his fift, and, it was on account of this expulfion, that he was not prefent at the chace of the Calydonian boar. From Calydon, he retired to the court of Ceyx, king of Trachinia; in his way he was ftopped by the fwollen ftreams of the Evenus, where the Centaur, Neffus, attempted to offer violence to Dejanira, under the perfidious pretence of conveying her over the river. Hercules perceived the diftrefs of Dejanira, and killed the Centaur with an arrow which had been dipt in the blood of the Lernæan Hydra. Neffus, as he expired, in order to avenge his death, gave Dejanira his tunic, which was covered with blood, poifoned and infected by the arrow; obferving, that it had the power of reclaiming a hufbund from unlawful love. Ceyx received Hercules with great marks of friendfhip, and purified him of the murder which he had committed at Calydon. Hercules was ftill mindful that he had been refufed the hand of Iole, and he therefore made war againft her father Eurytus, and killed him with three of his fons. Iole, who fell into the hands of the victor, found that fhe was beloved by him as much as ever. She accompanied him on Mount Œta, where he was going to raife an altar, and offer a folemn facrifice to Jupiter.

Jupiter. As he had not then the tunic in which he arrayed himself on thefe occafions, he fent Lichas to Dejanira, in order to provide himfelf with a fuitable drefs. Dejanira informed of her hufband's attachment for Iole, fent him the tunic which fhe had received from Neffus, and Hercules had no fooner put it on, than he found the poifon of the Lernæan Hydra penetrate through his bones. He attempted to tear off the fatal drefs, but it was already incorporated with his flefh, and in the midft of his pains and tortures, he uttered the moft bitter imprecations againft the credulous Dejanira, the cruelty of Euryftheus, and the jealoufy and hatred of Juno. He feized the unfortunate Lichas, who had brought him the tunic, and threw him into the fea with great violence, where he was changed by the Gods into a rock. As the diftemper of Hercules was incurable, he commended himfelf to Jupiter, and giving his bow and arrows to his friend Philoctetes, he erected a large pile on the top of Mount Œta; then fpreading on the pile the fkin of the Nemæan lion, he laid himfelf down upon it as on a bed, leaning his head upon his club. Philoctetes, or, according to others, Pæan, or Hyllus, was ordered to fet fire to the pile, and the hero faw himfelf on a fudden furrounded with the flames, without betraying any marks of fear or aftonifhment. Jupiter

N 4 beheld

beheld him, and announced to the surrounding
Deities, that he was about to elevate to the
skies, the immortal parts of a hero, who had
cleared the earth of so many monsters and ty-
rants. The Gods applauded Jupiter's resolu-
tion; the burning pile was suddenly encom-
passed with a thick smoke, and after the mortal
parts of Hercules were confumed, he was carried up into Heaven, in a chariot drawn by
four horses. Some loud claps of thunder accompanied his elevation, and his friends, unable
to find his ashes, shewed their gratitude to his
memory, by raising an altar where the pile had
stood. Menœtius, the son of Actor, offered
him a sacrifice of a bull, a wild boar, and a
goat, and enjoined the people of Opus, yearly,
to observe the same religious ceremonies. His
worship soon became as universal as his fame,
and Juno, who had once persecuted him with
such inveterate fury, forgot her resentments,
and gave him her daughter Hebe in marriage.
Hercules has received many firnames and epithets, either from the place where his worship
was established, or from the labours which he
atchieved. He was called Alcides, from Al-
cæus, the father of Amphitrion; he was likewife called Amphitryonides. His temples
were numerous and magnificent, and his divinity

vinity revered: No dogs or flies ever entered his temple at Rome; and that of Gades,
according to Strabo, was always forbidden
to women, and to pigs. The Phœnicians
offered quails on his altars; and as it was
suppofed he prefided over dreams, the fick
and infirm were fent to fleep in his temples,
that they might receive in their dreams, the
agreeable prefages of their recovery. The white
poplar was particularly dedicated to his fervice.
Hercules is ufually reprefented with ftrong and
well-proportioned limbs; he is fometimes covered with the fkin of the Nemæan lion, and
holds a noted club in his hand, on which he
leans; fometimes he appears crowned with the
leaves of the poplar, and holding the horn of
plenty under his arm; at other times, he is reprefented ftanding with Cupid, who infolently
breaks to pieces his arrows and his club, to intimate the power which the paffion of love had
over this hero, who fubmitted to be beaten and
ridiculed by Omphale, who dreffed herfelf in
his armour, while he was fitting to fpin with
her female fervants. Hercules was faid to have
fupported, for a while, the weight of the Heavens
upon his fhoulders, and to have feparated, by
the force of his arm, the two celebrated mountains of Abyla, on the coaft of Africa, and

N 5   Calpe,

Calpe, on the coast of Spain, which were supposed to have been formerly united, and placed
them at eighteen miles distance, opposite each
other; which separation made a communica-
tion between the Mediterranean and the Atlantic Ocean. These two mountains are called
the columns of Hercules, and were looked upon
as the boundaries of his labours. This hero is
held up by the Ancients as a model of virtue
and piety; and as his whole life had been employed for the common benefit of mankind, he
was thought to be deservedly rewarded with
immortality. His judicious choice of virtue, in
preference to pleasure, as described by Xenophon, is well known. The children of Hercules were as numerous as the labours and dif-
ficulties which he underwent, and they became
so powerful, soon after his death, that they alone
had the courage to invade all Peloponnesus: they
were called Heraclidæ, from their father; and
this name was common to all their descendants.
Hyllus, a son of Hercules and Dejanira, soon
after his father's death, married Iole: he, as
well as all his family, was persecuted by the
envy of Eurystheus, and obliged to fly from
Peloponnesus. The Athenians gave a kind reception to Hyllus, and the rest of the Heraclidæ, and marched against Eurystheus. Hyllus
                                         obtained

obtained a victory over his enemies; killed, with his own hand, Euryftheus, and fent his head to Alcmena, his grandmother. Some time after he attempted to recover the Peloponnefus, with the Heraclidæ, and was killed in fingle combat by Echemus, king of Arcadia. The defcendants of Hercules, after many unfuccefsful attempts for the recovery of the Peponnefus, became at laft mafters of all the peninfula. This conqueft makes an interefting epoch in ancient hiftory: it was finally atchieved about 120 years after the firft attempt of Hyllus, who was killed about twenty years before the Trojan war.

N 6 JASON

JASON.

JASON, a celebrated hero, son of Alcimede, daughter of Phylacus, by Æson, the son of Cretheus, and Tyro the daughter of Salmoneus. Tyro, before her connection with Cretheus, the son of Æolus, had two sons, Pelias and Neleus, by Neptune. Æson was king of Iolchos, and, at his death, the throne was usurped by Pelias, on account of the tender years of Jason, the rightful successor. The education of young Jason was entrusted to the Centaur Chiron, and he was removed from the presence of the usurper, who had been informed by an Oracle, that one of the descendants of Æolus would dethrone him. After Jason had made the most extraordinary progress in every branch of science, he quitted the Centaur, and, by his advice, went to consult the Oracle, where was ordered to return to his native country. He obeyed, and repairing to Iolchos, boldly demanded of Pelias, the kingdom which he had unjustly usurped from him. Pelias was intimidated by the spirit and intrepidity of the young

hero;

hero; yet unwilling to refign the crown, he fought to remove the immediate claim of Jafon, by exciting his thirft of glory, and reminded him, that Æetes, king of Colchis, had inhumanly murdered their common relation, Phryxus; he obferved, that fuch an action called aloud for punifhment, and that the undertaking would enfure immortal fame; he added, that his age and infirmities had alone prevented him from avenging the death of Phryxus, and that if Jafon would undertake the expedition, he would refign to him the crown of Iolchos, when he returned victorious from Colchis. Phryxus was fon of Athamas, King of Thebes, in Bœotia: he was a fon of Æolus, and had married Nephele, and fome time after, on pretence that fhe was fubject to fits of madnefs, he married Ino, who became jealous of the children of Nephele, becaufe they were to afcend their father's throne in preference to her own, and fhe refolved to deftroy them. Phryxus was apprized of Ino's intentions; and having fecured part of his father's treafures, privately left Bœotia, with his fifter Helle, to go to their friend and relation, Æetes, King of Colchis: they embarked on board a fhip, or, according to the more fabulous accounts of fome mythologifts, they mounted on the back

of

of a ram, whose fleece was of gold, and proceeded on their journey through the air. The
height to which they were carried, made Helle
giddy, and she fell into that part of the sea
which is called Hellefpont, from her name.
Phryxus continued his flight, and arrived safe
in the kingdom of Æetes, where he offered
the ram on the altar of Mars. The king
received him with great kindnefs, and gave
his daughter Chalciope in marriage. She had
by him two fons, Phrontis Melas, and Argos
Cylindrus, whom fome call Cytorus. Phryxus
was, however, fome time after, murdered by
his father-in-law, who envied him the poffeffion
of the golden fleece and Chalciope; who, to prevent her children from fharing the fate with
their father, fent them privately to Bœotia, as
they had not then any thing to fear from the
jealoufy of Ino, who had been changed into a
Sea-Deity. The fable of the flight of Phryxus
to Colchis, on a ram, has been explained by
fome, who obferve, that the fhip on which he
embarked, was either called by that name, or
carried on her prow the figure of that animal.
The fleece of gold is explained by the treafures
which Phryxus carried away from Thebes.
Phryxus was faid to have been placed among
the conftellations of Heaven after his death.
The

The ram which carried him to Afia, was faid to have been the fruit of Neptune's amour with Theophane. This ram, fay the Poets, had been prefented to Athamas, by the Gods, to reward his piety towards them, and Nephele procured it, to affift her children in their efcape from the jealous rage of Ino.

To return to our hero; he readily accepted a propofal which feemed to promife fuch military fame, and his intended expedition was no fooner made public, than all the youngeft and braveft of the Greeks affembled to accompany him, and to fhare his toils and glory. Among thefe were Hercules, Caftor and Pollux, fons of Jupiter. Acaftus the fon and Neleus, the brother, of Pelias, with Afterius, fon of Neleus; Orpheus and Amphion; Meleager and Atalanta, the daughter of Schœneus; Neftor, fon of Neleus, and Oileus, the father of Ajax; Philoctetes, the friend of Hercules; Thefeus, and his friend Pirithous; Æfculapius, fon of Apollo; Zethes and Calais, fons of Boreas; Deucalion, fon of Minos; Peleus and Telemon, fons of Æacus; Laertes, fon of Arcefius, and father of Ulyffes; and Argus, the builder of the fhip Argo, in which Jafon and his companions embarked, and from which they were called Argonauts.

gonauts. In their voyage they encountered
various and extraordinary adventures. They
stopped at the island of Lemnos, where they
remained some time, and raised a new race of
men, from the Lemnian women, who had
murdered their husbands, in revenge for their
infidelity. Jason had by Hypsipyle, the queen
of the country, twin sons, Euneus and Nebro-
phonus. After the Argonauts had left Lemnos,
they visited Samothrace, where they offered sacrifices to the Gods, and then passed to Troas,
and to Cyzicum. Here they met with a favourable reception; but Jason inadvertently
killed Cyzicus, the king of the country. To
expiate this murder, he buried Cyzicus with
great magnificence, offered a sacrifice to the
Mother of the Gods, to whom he built
a temple on Mount Dyndimus. From Cyzicum they visited Bithynia, where Pollux
accepted the challenge of Amycus, king
of the country, in the combat of the Cestus,
and slew him: they were afterwards driven
by a storm to Salmydessa, on the coast of
Thrace, where they delivered Phineus, the
king of the place, from the persecution of the
Harpyes. In the country of the Mariandini-
ans they lost two of their companions, Idmon
and Typhis, their pilot. After they had left
this

'this coaft, they were driven upon the ifland
of Arecia, where they found the children of
Phryxus, who had been fent by their mother
into Greece. From this ifland the Argonauts
arrived fafe in Æa, the capital of Colchis. Jafon explained the caufe of his voyage to Æetes,
but the conditions on which he was to recover
the golden fleece, were fo hard, that he muft
have perifhed in the attempt, had not Medea,
the king's daughter, become enamoured of him.
She met the leader of the Argonauts in the
temple of Hecate, where they exchanged mutual oaths of fidelity, and Medea promifed to
deliver Jafon from her father's hard conditions,
while he on his fide, engaged to marry, and
carry her with him to Greece. He was to tame
two bulls, which breathed flames, and which
had feet and horns of brafs, and to plough with
them a field facred to Mars. After this, he
was to fow in the ground the teeth of a ferpent, from which armed men would arife, whofe
fury would inftantly turn againft him who had
ploughed the field. He was alfo to kill a monftrous dragon, which watched night and day at
the foot of the tree on which the golden fleece
was fufpended. Medea, who was fkilled in the
knowledge of herbs, enchantments, and incantations, provided her lover with whatever herbs
and

and inftruments could protect him in the dangers
to which, he was going to be expofed. Thus
prepared, he appeared in the field of Mars; he
tamed the fury of the oxen, ploughed the plain,
and fowed the ferpent's teeth. Immediately an
army of men fprung from the earth, and ran
towards Jafon; he threw a ftone among them,
and they fell upon each other, till all were totally deftroyed. The vigilance of the dragon
was lulled to fleep by the power of herbs, and
Jafon took from the tree the celebrated golden
fleece, which was the fole object of his voyage.
Thefe actions were all performed in the prefence
of Æetes and his people, who were all equally
aftonifhed at the boldnefs and fuccefs of Jafon.
The hero, immediately after this conqueft, fet
fail for Europe with Medea, who had been fo
inftrumental in his prefervation. Æetes, defirous to revenge the perfidy of his daughter,
fent his fon Abfyrtus to purfue the fugitives.
Medea killed her brother, and ftrewed his limbs
in her father's way, that fhe might more eafily
efcape, while he was employed in collecting the
mangled members of his fon. The Argonauts,
on their return, came to the ifland of Peuceftes,
and to that of Circe, daughter of the Sun, who
refufed to purify them of the murder of Abfyrtus. They afterwards paffed the Straits of
Scylla and Charybdis, where they muft have
perifhed,

perifhed, had not the Sea-Goddefs, Thetis, preferved them, on account of her hufband Peleus,
who was one of the companions of Jafon : they
were delivered from the Sirens, by the melodious voice and lyre of Orpheus, and arrived in
the ifland of the Phæacians, where they met
the enemy's fleet, which had continued the
purfuit by a different courfe ; it was therefore
refolved, that Medea fhould be reftored, if fhe
had not been actually married to Jafon ; but
the wife of Alcinous, king of the country, being, appointed umpire between the Colchians
and Argonauts, had the marriage privately celebrated, and declared that the claims of Æetes
to Medea were now void. From Phæacia, the
Argonauts came to the Bay of Ambracia,
whence they were driven by a ftorm upon the
coaft of Africa ; and, after many difafters, at
laft came in fight of the promontory of Malea,
in the Peloponnefus, where they were purified
of the murder of Abfyrtus, and foon after arrived fafe in Theffaly, where their return was
celebrated with univerfal feftivity. Some mythologifts fay, that Æfon, the father of Jafon,
was not dead, when his fon undertook the Argonautic expedition ; but that he had been difpoffeffed by Pelias, and that he was ftill alive
when Jafon returned victorious. Thefe authors
add,

add, that Medea, by her art, reftored Æfon, who was grown old and infirm, to the vigour and fprightlinefs of youth. Pelias wifhing likewife to fee himfelf reftored to the flower of youth, his daughters, perfuaded by Medea, who was defirous of avenging her hufband's wrongs, put him in a cauldron of boiling water. Their credulity was feverely punifhed; Medea fuffered the flefh to be confumed, and Pelias was never reftored to life. This inhuman action drew the refentment of the populace upon Medea, and fhe fled with Jafon to Corinth, where they remained fome years; but their conjugal felicity was at length difturbed, by a paffion which Jafon conceived for Glauce, daughter of the king of the country; and in order to marry her, he divorced Medea, who, in revenge for her hufband's infidelity, prefented Glauce with a poifoned garment, which fhe had no fooner put on, than it fet fire to her body, and fhe expired in the moft excruciating torments. This victim, however, could not fatisfy the jealous rage of Medea; and, in her mad tranfports, fhe killed two of her own children, in the prefence of their father; and when Jafon attempted to punifh her for this barbarity, fhe fled from him through the air, on a chariot drawn by winged dragons. Jafon, fome time

after

after his separation from Medea, was one day reposing himself by the side of the ship which had carried him to Colchis, when a beam fell upon his head, and crushed him to death. This tragical event had been predicted to him long before, by Medea, according to some authors; but others say, that Jason returned to Colchis, where he again met with Medea, and was reconciled to her, and that they reigned there together in peace and security. The Argonautic expedition, according to the best calculations, was atchieved about thirty-five years before the Trojan war. It has employed the pen of many of the writers of antiquity; among the historians, Diodorus Siculus, Strabo, Apollodorus, and Justin; and among the Poets, Onamacritus, more generally called Orpheus, Apollonius Rhodius, Pindar and Valerius Flaccus, have all related its most remarkable particulars.

THESEUS.

THESEUS.

THESEUS, king of Athens, and son of Ægeus, by Æthra, the daughter of Pittheus, was one of the most celebrated of the heroes of antiquity. He was educated at Træzene, in the house of Pittheus, and, and as he was not publickly acknowledged to be the son of the king of Athens, he passed for the son of Neptune. When he came to years of maturity, he was sent by his mother to Athens, and a sword was given him; by means of which he might privately make himself known to his father. On the road Theseus met with many perilous adventures, occasioned by the robbers and wild beasts with which those parts were infested, but all these obstacles were surmounted by the intrepid hero. He destroyed Corynetes, Synnis, Sciron, Procustes, Cercyon, and the celebrated Phæa, from whom the boar of Calydon was said to spring. Theseus, however, did not meet with a cordial reception at Athens. Medea, who had taken refuge at that court, after she had fled from the resentment of Jason, had

great

great influence over the mind of Ægeus, which
fhe feared to lofe, if Thefeus was acknowledged his fon; fhe therefore attempted to deftroy
this unwelcome heir, before his arrival was
made public. Ægeus himfelf was to give the
cup of poifon to the unknown gueft at the
feaft, but the fight of his fword by the fide of
Thefeus, reminded him of his amours with
Æthra, with whom he had left this fword, and
enjoined her, if fhe had a fon, to give it to him
when he fhould be of a proper age, and fend
him to Athens. Ægeus, by this token, knew
his fon, and publicly acknowledged him; and
his people rejoiced to find that this illuftrious
hero, who had cleared Attica from robbers
and pirates, was born to reign over them. The
Pallantides, who had expected to fucceed their
uncle Ægeus on the throne, attempted to af-
faffinate Thefeus; but they fell in their own
fnares, and were all put to death by the
young prince. The bull of Marathon next engaged the hero's attention; the labour feemed
arduous, but he caught the animal alive, and
after he had led it throhgh the ftreets of Athens,
he facrificed it to Minerva, or the God of Delphi. After this, Thefeus went to Crete, among
the feven chofen youths, whom the Athenians

were

were obliged to send thither every year, to be devoured by the Minotaur. The wish to deliver the country from so dreadful a tribute, engaged him to undertake this dangerous expedition. Minos, second king of Crete, had imposed this hard condition upon the Athenians, after having obtained a victory over them, because his son Androgeus had been slain in the battle; he likewise obliged them to send yearly seven young virgins, who were sacrificed at the same time, to the monster. The Minotaur was half a man and half a bull, said to be the fruit of the indecent amours of Pasiphae, the wife of Minos. The king had received from Neptune a beautiful white bull, with orders to sacrifice it on his altar. Minos, pleased with the animal, resolved to preserve it, and the God, to punish his disobedience, caused Pasiphae to be enamoured of this fine bull. The fabulous tradition of the poets, who pretend that the Minotaur was the fruit of this infamous connection, is refuted by some writers, who suppose that the infidelity of Pasiphae to her husband, was occasioned by an affection which she had conceived for one of his officers, named Taurus, and that Dædalus, who built the famous labyrinth of Crete, by permitting his house to be the asylum of the lovers, was looked

upon

upon as acceffary to the crime of Pafiphæ. Minos confined him in the labyrinth which he had
conftructed. Here he made wings with feathers and wax, and fitted them to his body, and
that of his fon Icarus, who was the companion
of his confinement. They took their flight in
the air, from Crete, but the heat of the fun,
melted the wax on the wings of Icarus, whofe
flight was too high, and he fell into that part of
the ocean, which from him, has been called the
Icarian fea. The father, by a proper management of his wings, alighted Cumæ, where he
built a temple to Apollo, and thence directed
is courfe towards Sicily; where he was kindly
received by Cocalus, who reigned over part of
the country.

Thefeus, on his arrival in Crete, was fhut up
in the Labyrinth where the Minotaur was kept,
to be devoured by him, but having the good
fortune to pleafe Ariadne, the King's daughter,
he killed the monfter, and efcaped from the La-
byrith, by means of a clue of thread, which fhe
gave him, and without which it was impoffible
to find the way through the perplexed windings
of the edifice. Thefeus immediately failed from
Crete, with his companions, whom he had redeemed from death by this victory. Ariadne

O   likewife

likewise accompanied him in his flight, but he
had the cruelty to abandon her to whom he
owed his safety, and left her, while she was
asleep, in the island of Naxos, where they had
been driven by contrary winds. In this discon-
solate situation she was found by Bacchus, who
married her, and gave her a crown of seven
stars, which was placed among the constella-
tions, after the death of Ariadne. The ships
in which Theseus had sailed from Athens, had
black sails, and he had promised his father to
change them for white ones, if he returned victorious; he had, however, forgotten to take this
precaution, and Ægeus, who watched continually for the return of the vessel, no sooner
beheld the black sails, which he regarded as the
certain signal of ill-success, than he threw himself in despair, from a high rock into the sea.
Theseus ascended the throne, and was adored
by his subjects, for the equity and mildness of
his reign. The fame which he had acquired by
his victories and policy, made his alliance
courted by the neighbouring princes, but Pirithous, son of Ixion, and king of the Lapithæ,
wished to meet him in the field of battle. He
accordingly invaded Attica, and when Theseus had marched out to meet him, the two enemies, struck at the sight of each other, rushed
between

between their two armies, to embrace in the
moft cordial and affectionate manner, and from
that time began the moft fincere and admired
friendſhip, which has become proverbial. Thefeus was prefent at the nuptials of his friend,
and he was the moft eager and courageous of
the Lapithæ in the defence, of Hippodamia,
and her female attendants, from the brutal attempts of the Centaurs. Hercules was likewife prefent; and did not fail to diftinguſh himfelf on this occafion, on behalf of the women.
This is the famous battle of the Centaurs with
the Lapithæ, which is elegantly defcribed by
Ovid, and has likewife employed the pen of Hefiod, Valerius Flaccus, &c. The Centaurs
were defeated, and obliged to retire into Arcadia, where their infolence was a fecond time
puniſhed by Hercules, when he was going to
hunt the boar of Erymanthus. Thefeus married Hippolyte, queen of the Amazons, by whom
he had a fon, named Hippolitus. After her
death he married Phædra, the fifter of Ariadne,
by whom he had Acamas and Demophoon.
They had long lived in conjugal felicity, when
Venus, who hated all the defcendants of the
fun, infpired Phædra with an unconquerable
paffion for Hippolytus, whom ſhe addreffed on
the fubject of this criminal fondnefs. The
young

prince, filled with horror, rejected her with dif-
dain, and Phædra, incensed beyond measure at
this reception, resolved to punish his coldness
and refusal; she therefore accused him to Theseus of having attempted her virtue. The
credulous father believed the accusation, and
without hearing the defence of Hippolytus, he
banished him from his kingdom, and implored
Neptune, who had promised to grant him three
requests, to punish him in some exemplary
manner; accordingly, as the unfortunate Prince
fled from Athens, his horses were suddenly terrified by a huge sea-monster, which Neptune
had sent on the shore. He was dragged
through precipices, and over rocks, and was
trampled under the feet of his own horses, and
crushed by the wheels of his chariot. When
the tragical fate of Hippolytus was known at
Athens, Phædra confessed her crime, and killed
herself, unable to survive him whose death her
guilt had occasioned. The death of Hippolytus,
and the incestuous passion of Phædra, is the subject of one of the tragedides of Euripides, and of
Seneca. Helen, according to some writers,
was carried away, when very young, by Theseus
aided by Pirithous, and they even add, that she
had a daughter by him; but the resentment of
Castor and Pollux soon obliged him to restore

ftore her into their hands ; all this ftory is however confuted by other Mythologifts. Some
Some fay that Thefeus and his friend defcended
into the Infernal Regions, with an intention to
carry away Proferpine ; but Pluto, apprized of
their defign, prevented them. To punifh their
bold attempt, Pirithous was placed on his father's wheel, and Thefeus was faftened to a
huge ftone, on which he had fat to repofe himfelf. Some time after, Hercules delivered the
two friends from their confinement and torments, and they were permitted to return upon
earth with him, when he came to fetch the dog
Cerberus ; and he redeemed likewife Alcefte,
the daughter of Pelias, who had voluntarily
fubmitted to death herfelf, to fave the life of
her hufband Admretus. During the captivity of
Thefeus in the kingdom of Pluto, Mneftheus,
a defcendant of Erectheus, ingratiated himfelf
into the favour of the people of Athens, and
obtained the crown in preference to the children of the abfent monarch. Thefeus, at
his return, endeavoured in vain to eject the
ufurper. The Athenians had forgotton all his
benefits, and he was obliged to retire to the
court of Lycomedes, king of the ifland of Sciros.
Lycomedes, after paying him much attention,
growing jealous of his fame, or bribed by the

prefents

prefents of Mneftheus, took him to the top of
a high rock, on pretence of fhewing him the
extent of his dominions, and threw him down
a deep precipice. Some fuppofe that Thefeus
inadvertently fell down this precipice, and was
crufhed to death, without receiving any violence 'from Lycomedes. After the death of
Mneftheus, the children of Thefeus recovered
the throne of Athens, and, that the memory of
their father might receive the honours due to a
hero, they brought his remains from Scyros,
and gave them a magnificent burial: they alfo
raifed ftatues and a temple, and feftivals and
games were inftituted, to commemorate the
actions of a hero, who had rendered fuch fervices to the people of Athens. Thefe feftivals
were ftill celebrated with original folemnity in
the age of Paufanias and Plutarch, about 1200
years after the death of Thefeus. The hiftorians difagree with the poets in their accounts
of this hero, and they fuppofe that it was not
the Queen of Hell, but Proferpine, the daughter of Aidoneus, a king of the Moloffi, whom
they attempted to take away by force. The dog,
which kept the gates of the palace, was, they
fay, called Cerberus, and, from this fimilitude
of names, perhaps, arifes the fiction of the
poets. Pirithous was torn in pieces by the dog,
and

and Thefeus was confined in a prifon, from whence he made his efcape, by the affiftance of Hercules. Some authors fay, that thefe friends were not of the number of the number of the Argonauts; but that they were both detained either in the country of the Moloffi, or in the Infernal Regions, at the time of Jafon's expedition to Colchis.

PERSEUS.

PERSEUS.

PERSEUS, fon of Jupiter and Danae, the daughter of Acrifius, whofe birth gave fuch uneafinefs to his grand-father, on account of the oracle, which had foretold, that he was to perifh by the hand of his daughter's fon, that he caufed both the child and its mother to be thrown into fea: they were, however, preferved by a fifher-man, called Dictys, and carried to Polydectes, King of the ifland of Seriphos, one of the Cyclades, who treated them with great humanity, and Perfeus was entrufted to the care of the priefts of Minerva. His rifing genius and courage, however, foon began to difpleafe Polydectes, who had conceived a paffion for Danae; and, as the prefence of her fon feemed an obftacle to its gratification, he refolved to remove him, by engaging him in fome perilous enterprize, in which he hoped he might perifh; he therefore required of Perfeus, to bring him the head of the Gorgon Medufa. The young hero did not decline the arduous undertaking, and by the favour of the Gods, and particularly by

the

the affiftance of Minerva, who peculiarly patronized him, he happily atchieved this celebrated
conqueft, in the manner that has been already
related in the account which has been given of
the Gorgons. The conqueror, on his return,
ftopped at the palace of Atlas, King of Mau-
ritania, brother to Prometheus, where he hoped
to meet a kind reception, by announcing himfelf as the fon of Jupiter, but his hopes were
difappointed. Atlas recollected that, according
to an ancient oracle, his gardens were to be
robbed of their fruit, by a fon of Jupiter, and,
therefore, he not only refufed Perfeus the hofpitality he demanded, but he even attempted to
offer violence to his perfon. Perfeus, as his beft
means of defence, fhewed him the head of Medufa, and inftantly Atlas was changed into a
large mountain, which bore his name, in the
defarts of Africa. Perfeus, after this, continued his flight through the air, mounted on the
winged horfe Pegafus, which had fprung from
the blood of Medufa; and, as he paffed through
the territories of Libya, he difcovered on the
coafts of Æthiopia, the beautiful Andromeda,
expofed to a fea-monfter. She was daughter
to Cepheus, King of Æthiopia, by Caffiope,
and had been promifed in marriage to her uncle
Phineus, when Neptune fent an inundation

into

into the kingdom, and a fea-monfter to ravage
the country, becaufe Caffiope had boafted herfelf fairer than Juno and the Nereides. The
oracle of Jupiter Ammon had pronounced, that
Andromeda muft be expofed to be devoured
by the monfter, and that this facrifice alone
could appeafe the offended Deities: fhe was
accordingly chained to a rock, and, at the
moment the monfter was about to feize his
prey, Perfeus appeared. He had been ftruck
with her charms, and touched by her fituation,
and offered her father to deliver her from death,
provided he might obtain her in marriage, as
the reward of his labours. Cepheus did not
hefitate to promife what he required, and immediately the hero, raifing himfelf in the air,
flew towards the monfter, and holding full before his eyes, the petrifying head which he carried, inftantly turned him into a rock. This
happy event was celebrated with great feftivity,
and Andromeda was the fame day given in
marriage to her deliverer, who raifed three
altars to Jupiter, Mercury, and Pallas, on which
he offered facrifices, as a teftimony of his gratitude to thofe Deities, for the protection they
had afforded him. The univerfal joy was,
however, difturbed by Phineus, the uncle of
Andromeda, who entered the palace with a
number

number of armed men, and attempted to carry
away the bride. Perſeus, in oppoſing this violence, muſt have fallen a victim to the rage of
Phineus, had he not at laſt had recourſe to the
ſame arms, which had already proved ſo fatal
to Atlas and the ſea-monſter. He ſhewed the
Gorgon's head to his adverſaries, and they were
inſtantly turned to ſtone ; each in the ſame at-
titude in which he then ſtood. Cepheus, and
all thoſe who had ſupported Perſeus, ſhared not
the fate of Phineus and his adherents, the hero
having previouſly warned them of the power of
the terrific head. Soon after this memorable
adventure, Perſeus returned to Seriphos, at the
very moment that his mother Danae fled to the
altar of Minerva, to avoid the purſuit of Polydectes, who attempted to offer her violence.
Dictys, who had ſaved her from the ſea, and
who, as ſome ſay, was the brother of Polydectes,
defended her valiantly, and therefore Perſeus,
ſenſible of his merit and humanity, placed him
on the throne of Seriphos, after he had puniſhed
Polydectes, and the aſſociates of his guilt, by
turning them into ſtones. Perſeus, after this,
wiſhing to reviſit his native country, embarked
for the Peloponneſus, with his mother and
Andromeda. When he reached thoſe coaſts,
he was informed, that Tutamias, King of La-

O 6   riſſa,

riffa, was celebrating funeral games, in honour of his father. This intelligence drew him to Lariffa, to fignalize himfelf in throwing the quoit, of which, according to fome, he was the inventor; but here he was fo unfortunate as to kill a man with a quoit which he had thrown in the air. This man was no other than his grandfather, Acrifius, who, on hearing that his grandfon was arrived in the Peloponnefus, had immediately fled from his kingdom of Argos, to the court of his friend and ally Teutamias, to prevent the fulfilling of the oracle, which had induced him to treat his daughter and her child with fo much feverity. Some fuppofe, that Acrifius had gone to Lariffa, to be reconciled to his grandfon, whofe fame had been fpread in every city of Greece, and Ovid maintains, that Perfeus had re-inftated his grandfather in his kingdom, from which he had been forcibly driven by the fons of his brother, Proetus, before the unfortunate accident of the quoit. Perfeus was greatly afflicted at having occafioned the death of Acrifius; and though by it he became entitled to the throne of Argos, he re-fufed to reign there, and, in order to remove from a place, which reminded him of the par-ricide which he had involuntarily committed, he exchanged his kingdom for that of Tirynthus, and

and the maritime coaſt of Argolis, where Me-
gapenthes, the ſon of Prœtus, then reigned.
When he had finally ſettled in this part of the
Peloponneſus, he determined to lay the foundation of a new city, which he made the capital of his dominions, and called it Mycenæ.
The time and manner of the death of Perſeus,
are not known, but it is univerſally agreed, that
he received divine honours, like the reſt of the
ancient heroes. He had ſtatues at Mycenæ,
and in the iſland of Seriphos, and the Athenians raiſed him a temple, in which they con-
ſecrated an altar to Dictys, who had treated
Danae and her infant ſon with ſuch paternal tenderneſs. The Egyptians alſo paid
particular honour to the memory of this hero,
and aſſerted, that he ſometimes appeared
among them, wearing ſhoes two cubits long,
which was always interpreted as a ſign of fer-
tility. Perſeus had by Andromeda, Alceus,
Sthenelus, Neſtor, Electryon, and Gorgophone.
After his death, according to ſome mythologiſts, he became a conſtellation in the Heavens.

ULYSSES.

ULYSSES.

Ulysses, king of the iſlands of Ithaca and Dulichium, ſon of Anticlea, the daughter of Autolycus, and of Laertes; though ſome authors ſay, that Siſyphus was his father, yet he was generally reputed the ſon of Laertes. He was one of the ſuitors of Helen, but, as he deſpaired of ſucceſs in his applications, on account of the great number of Princes who ſolicited her hand, he demanded Penelope, the daughter of Icarius, in marriage, and obtained her by means of Tyndarus, the reputed father of Helen, who was uncle to Penelope, and who had been adviſed by Ulyſſes, to permit his daughter an uninfluenced choice among her ſuitors, and to bind them all by a ſolemn oath, to unite together in protecting her perſon, if any violence ſhould ever be offered to her. All the contending Princes ſubmitted to this deciſion, and Helen choſe Menelaus. Ulyſſes, after this, returned to Ithaca, where his father reſigned to him the crown, and retired to peace and rural ſolitude. But the rape of Helen, by Paris,

Paris, did not allow Ulyſſes long to enjoy a happineſs which ſeemed ſo perfect. He was ſummoned to the war, with the other Princes of Greece. Unwilling to leave his kingdom, and his beloved Penelope, whoſe virtues and tenderneſs were without example, he pretended to be inſane, and. he yoked a horſe and a bull together, with which he ploughed the ſea-ſhore, where he ſowed ſalt inſtead of corn. The deceit was ſoon diſcovered by Palamedes, a Grecian chief, who was ſent to bring Ulyſſes to meet the aſſembled Princes; he took Telemachus, whom Penelope had lately brought into the world, and laid him before the plough of his father, who diſcovered that his inſanity was not real, by turning the plough a different way, to avoid hurting his infant ſon. Ulyſſes was therefore obliged to go to the Trojan war, where he ſoon diſtinguiſhed himſelf by his valour, and ſtill more by his prudence and ſagacity. By his means Achilles was diſcovered among the daughters of Lycomedes, king of Scyros, and Philoctetus was induced to abandon Lemnos, and to bring the arrows of Hercules to the ſiege of Troy. With the aſſiſtance of Diomedes, he ſlew Rheſus, and the ſleeping Thracians, in the midſt of their camp, and he introduced himſelf into the city of Priam,

and

and carried away the palladium of the Trojans. For thefe eminent fervices he was held in the higheft eftimation among the Greeks; and, after the death of Achilles, was rewarded with his arms, for the poffeffion of which, Ajax had contended with him. After the deftruction of Troy, Ulyffes embarked to return to Greece; but he was expofed to a number of misfortunes before he reached his native country, from which he was abfent twenty years. It feems, however, unneceffary here, to enter into the particulars of thofe adventures, which are fo fully and beautifully defcribed in the Odeffey of Homer, a poem fo univerfally read and admired. Suffice it to fay, that the hero at laft arrived happily at Ithaca, where, after having punifhed with death all the infolent fuitors of his wife Penelope, by whom fhe had been perfecuted during his abfence, he reigned in peace many years. It is faid, that he was at laft killed by Telegonus, a fon whom he had had by the for-cerefs Circe, and who had landed in Ithaca, in hopes of making himfelf known to his father, whom he flew in a quarrel, without knowing who he was.

ACHILLES.

ACHILLES.

ACHILLES, son of Peleus and Thetis, was the bravest of all the Greeks who went to the Trojan war. He was, as has been said, invulnerable in every part, except the heel, by which his mother held him, when she plunged him in the Stygian Lake. He was educated by the Centaur Chiron, who taught him the art of war, and made him master of music, and by feeding him with the marrow of wild beasts, rendered him vigorous and active. He was taught eloquence by Phœnix, whom he ever after loved and respected. Thetis, to prevent her son from going to the siege of Troy, where he was doomed to perish, privately sent him to the court of Lycomedes, where he was disguised in a female dress; but as Troy could not be taken without the aid of Achilles, Ulysses undertook to bring him to the Grecian camp; he went to the court of Lycomedes, in the habit of a merchant, and exposed jewels and arms to sale. Achilles, without regarding the shining baubles, which engaged the attention of his

female

female companions, eagerly feized and fitted on a fuit of armour. The penetration of the king of Ithaca needed no further proof that he had found Achilles, and he engaged him without difficulty, to depart with him for Troy. The actions of this hero, during that famous war ; . his quarrel with Agamemnon; his triumph over Hector; and his death by Paris, who wounded him in his vulnerable heel, are all related at large in the Iliad and Odeffey of Homer.' Achilles was buried at Sigæum, and divine honours were paid to him, and temples raifed to his memory. The Theffalians yearly facrificed a black and a white bull on his tomb. It is faid, that when this hero was very young, he was afked by his mother, whether he fhould prefer a long life fpent in obfcurity and retirement, or a few years of military fame and glory, and that he made choice of the latter. Some ages after the Tro-jan war, Alexander, going to the conqueft of Perfia, offered facrifices on the tomb of Achilles, and admired the hero, who had found a Homer to publifh his fame to pofterity. Neoptolemus, called likewife Pyrrhus, was the fon of Achilles, by Deidamia, a daughter of Lycomedes. He was at the taking of Troy, and Priam fell by his hand.

ÆNEAS.

ÆNEAS.

ÆNEAS, a Trojan prince, fon of Anchifes, and the Goddefs Venus. He married Creufa, a daughter of Priam, by whom he had a fon called Afcanius. The opinions of authors concerning the character of Æneas are extremely different. During the Trojan war he behaved with great valour in defence of his country, and came to an engagement with Diomedes and Achilles; yet many writers accufe him of betraying Troy to the Greeks, with Antenor, and of preferving his life and fortune by that treachery. When Troy was in flames he carried away, upon his fhoulders, his father Anchifes, and the ftatues of his houfhold Gods, leading his young fon by the hand; but his wife, who followed behind, was killed by the Greeks. Some however fay, that fhe was faved by Cybele, who carried her away to her temple, of which fhe became the prieftefs. Æneas retired to Mount Ida, where he built a fleet of twenty fhips, and fet fail in queft of a fettlement. He directed his courfe towards Italy, whither he

was

was called by the will of the Gods, who had
promifed that he fhould there find a kingdom,
in which his pofterity fhould reign after him.
The various adventures which he encountered
during this voyage, is the fubject of the Æneid
of Virgil, which is fo generally known, that it
would be fuperfluous to relate them here. After enduring feven years of fatigues and dangers, which had elapfed fince he quitted his
native country, he arrived in Italy, and having
vanquifhed the enemies who oppofed his efta-
blifhment, he married Lavinia, daughter of the
king of the country, in whofe honour he built
the town of Lavinium, and fucceeded his father-
in-law.   After a fhort reign Æneas was killed
in a battle againft the Etrurians. Some fay
that he was drowned in the Numicus, where
his body was weighed down by his armour,
upon which the Latins, not finding their king,
fuppofed that he had been taken up to Heaven,
and therefore offered him facrifices as to a God.
The arrival of Æneas in Italy, has been fixed in
the 54th Olympiad. Some authors fuppofe, that
Æneas, after the fiege of Troy, fell to the fhare
of Neoptolemus, together with Andromache,
and that he was carried to Theffaly, whence he
efcaped to Italy.   Others fay, that after he had
come to Italy, he returned to Troy, which he
rebuilt,

rebuilt, leaving Afcanius king of Latium.
Æneas is reprefented as remarkable for his piety
and fubmiffion to the will of the Gods : he is
faid to have had a fon by Lavinia, called Syl-
vius, becaufe his mother retired with him into
the woods, after the death of his father, and
that he fucceeded Afcanius on the throne of
Latium.

CADMUS.

[CADMUS.

CADMUS, a fon of Agenor, king of Phœnicia. He was fent by his father in fearch of
his fifter Europa, whom Jupiter had carried
away, with orders never to return to Phœnicia,
if he did not bring her back. As his fearch
proved fruitlefs, he confulted the oracle of
Apollo, and was directed to build a city, where
he fhould fee a young heifer ftop in the grafs,
and to call the country Bœotia. He found the
heifer, according to the inftructions of the
oracle, and, as he wifhed to thank the God by
a facrifice, he fent his companions to fetch water
from a neighbouring grove. The waters were
facred to Mars, and guarded by a dragon, which
devoured all the defcendants of Cadmus, who,
tired with their feeming delay, went to the
place, and faw the monfter ftill feeding on their
flefh. He attacked the dragon, and overcame
it by the affiftance of Minerva, and fowed the
teeth in a plain, when fuddenly, armed men arofe
from the ground. Cadmus threw a ftone in
the midft of them, and they inftantly turned
their

their arms one against the other, till all perished, except five, who affisted him in the building of his city. ˉSoon after he married Hermione, the daughter of Venus, by whom he
had a fon, Polydorus, and four daughters, Ino,
Agave, Autonoe, and Semele. Polydorus married Nycteis, by whom he had Labdacus, the
father of Laius. All this family was perfecuted
by Juno with unrelented hatred, as has been already obferved. Cadmus and Hermione, overwhelmed by their own, and their childrens, mif-
fortunes, retired to Illyricum: they at laft entreated the Gods to remove them from the calamities of life, and they were changed into ferpents. Some explain the fable of the dragon,
by fuppofing that it was a king of the country,
who was conquered by Cadmus, and the armed
men rifing from the field, no more than men
armed with brafs, according to the fignification
of a Phœnician word. Cadmus was the firft
who introduced the ufe of letters in Greece; but
fome maintain, that the alphabet which he brought
from Phœnicia, was only different from that
which was ufed by the ancient inhabitants of
Greece. This alphabet confifted only of fix-
teen letters, to which Palamedes afterwards
added four, and Simonedes, of Melos, the fame
number. The worfhip of many of the Egyptian
and

and Phœnician Deities, was also brought into Greece by Cadmus. It is supposed that he lived about 1590 years before the Christian æra. According to those who say, that Thebes was built at the sound of Amphion's lyre, Cadmus built only a small citadel, which he called Cadmea, and laid the foundations of a city, which was afterwards finished under his successors.

CASTOR

CASTOR AND POLLUX.

CASTOR and Pollux, the twin fons of Leda, the wife of Tyndarus; the manner of their birth has been already related; they were both commonly called the fons of Jupiter, though Pollux alone was immortal. Mercury, immediately after their birth, carried them to Pallena, where they were educated, and, as foon as they had arrived to years of maturity, they embarked with Jafon, to go in queft of the golden fleece. In this expedition both behaved with fuperior courage. Pollux conquered and flew Amycus, in the combat of the Ceftus, and was ever after reckoned the God and Patron of Wreftlers. Caftor diftinguifhed himfelf in the management of horfes: they cleared the Hellefpont, and the neighbouring feas, from pirates, after their return from Colchis; from which circumftance, they were always deemed the friends of navigation. During the Argonautic expedition, in a violent ftorm, lambent flames were feen to play round the heads of the fons of Leda, and immediately the tempeft ceafed, and the fea was

P   calmed.

calmed. From this occurrence their power
to protect mariners has been more fully credited; and the two mentioned fires, which are
said to be common in storms, have since been
known by the name of Castor and Pollux.
When they both appeared, it was a sign of fair
weather; but if only one was seen, it prognos-
ticated storms, and was called Helena. Castor
and Pollux being invited to a feast, when
Lynceus and Idas were going to celebrate their
marriage with Phœbe and Talaira, the daughters of Leucippus, who was brother to Tindarus, they became enamoured of the two
women whose nuptials they came to celebrate,
and resolved to carry them away by force. This
violence provoked Lynceus and Idas, a battle
ensued, and Castor killed Lynceus, and was
killed by Idas. Pollux revenged the death of
his brother by that of Idas; but the loss of his
beloved Castor was so insupportable to him,
that he entreated Jupiter to restore his brother
to life, or to deprive himself of immortality.
Jupiter at length consented that Castor should
share it with him, and consequently, so long as
the one was upon earth, so long was the other
detained in the Infernal Regions, and they alternately lived and died every day; or, according to some, every six months. This act of
fraternal

fraternal love Jupiter rewarded, by making the two brothers conftellations in Heaven, under the name of Gemini, which never appear together, but when one rifes, the other fets, and fo on alternately. Caftor had a fon named Anogon, by Talaira; and Phœbe had Mnefileus, by Pollux. The brothers received divine honours, and white lambs were ufually offered on their altars: they were generally called Diofcuri, fons of Jupiter, and the Ancients frequently fwore by their divinity. Among the Romans there prevailed many reports at different times that Caftor and Pollux had made their appearance in the armies of that people; and, mounted on white fteeds, at the head of their troops, had furioufly attacked the enemy: they were generally reprefented mounted on white horfes, armed with fpears, and riding fide by fide, with their heads covered with a bonnet, on whofe top glittered a ftar.

ORPHEUS.

ORPHEUS, the fon of Apollo and the Mufe Calliope; though, by fome, he is faid to be the fon of Œager, a king of Thrace. He received a lyre from Apollo, or from Mercury, upon which he played with fuch a mafterly hand, that even the moft rapid rivers ceafed to flow, the favage beafts of the foreft forgot their ferocity, and the mountains came to liften to his fong. All nature feemed charmed and animated. Orpheus was beloved and followed by all the Nymphs; but Eurydice alone had been able to make an impreffion on his heart. He married her, but their happinefs was of fhort duration. Ariftæus became enamoured of Euridice, and as fhe fled from his importunities, a ferpent, which was lurking in the grafs, bit her foot, and fhe died of the poifoned wound. Her lofs was feverely felt by Orpheus, and he refolved to recover her, or perifh in the attempt. With his lyre in his hand, he entered the Infernal Regions, and gained admiffion to the palace of Pluto, who was charmed with the

melody

melody of his ftrains; and, according to the beautiful expreffions of the poets, the wheel of Ixion ftopped; the ftone of Sifyphus ftood ftill; Tantalus forgot his perpetual thirft, and even the Furies relented. Pluto and Proferpine were moved with his forrow, and confented to re-ftore him Eurydice, provided he forbore look-ing behind him, till he had paffed the extremeft borders of Hell. The conditions were gladly accepted, and Orpheus was already in fight of the Upper Regions, when he forgot his pro-mifes, and turned back to look at his long loft Eurydice. He faw her, but fhe inftantly va-nifhed from his eyes. He attempted to follow her, but he was refufed admiffion, and the fole confolation he could find, was to footh his grief by the found of his mufical inftrument in grot-toes, or on the mountains. He totally fepa-rated himfelf from the fociety of mankind, and the Thracian women, whom he had offended by his neglect and coldnefs towards them, at-tacked him, while they were celebrating the Orgies of Bacchus; and, after they had torn his body in pieces, they threw his head into the Hebrus, which ftill articulated the words Eu-rydice! Eurydice! as it was carried down the ftream into the Ægean Sea. Orpheus was one of the Argonauts, of which celebrated expedition

pedition he wrote a poetical account, still extant. This is doubted by Ariſtotle, who ſays,
according to Cicero, that there never exiſted
an Orpheus, but that the poems which paſs
under his name, are the compoſitions of a Py-
thagorean philoſopher, named Cercops. According to ſome of the Moderns, the Argonau-
tica, and the other poems attributed to Orpheus, are the production of the pen of Ono-
macritus, a poet, who lived in the age of Piſiſ-
tratus, tyrant of Athens. Pauſanias, however,
and Diodorus Siculus, ſpeak of Orpheus as a
great poet and muſician, who rendered himſelf
equally celebrated by his knowledge of the art
of war, by the extent of his underſtanding,
and by the laws which he enacted. Some maintain that he was killed by a thunder-bolt. He
was buried at Pieria, in Macedonia, according
to Apollodorus. The inhabitants of Dion
boaſted that his tomb was in their city, and the
people of Mount Libethrus, in Thrace, claimed
the ſame honour. Orpheus, as ſome report,
after death, received divine honours. The
Muſes gave an honourable burial to his remains,
and his lyre became one of the conſtellations in
the Heavens.

AMPHION.

AMPHION.

AMPHION, another mufician, much celebrated by the Ancients, was the fon of Jupiter
and Antiope, the daughter of Nycteus, who
had married Lycus, and had been repudiated
by him when he married Dirce. Amphion was
born at the fame birth with Zethus, on Mount
Cytheron, where Antiope had fled to avoid the
refentment of Dirce, from whom fhe experienced the moft barbarous treatment. The two
children were expofed in the woods, but preferved by a fhepherd. Amphion, as he grew
up, cultivated Poetry, and made fuch an uncommon progrefs in mufic, that he is, by fome,
faid to be the inventor of it, and to have built
the walls of Thebes at the found of his lyre.
Mercury taught him to play on this inftrument,
which he gave him, and Amphion was the firft
who raifed an altar to this God. Zethus and
Amphion united to avenge the wrongs which
their mother had fuffered from the cruelty of
Dirce. They befieged Lycus in his palace,
took him, and put him to death, and tied Dirce

to the tail of a wild bull, which dragged her through precipices till she expired. The fable of Amphion's moving stones, and raising the walls of Thebes at the sound of his lyre, has been explained, by supposing, that he persuaded, by his eloquence, a wild and uncivilized people to unite together, and build a town, in order to protect themselves from the attacks of their enemies.

F I N I S.

4. A NEW COMPENDIOUS GRAMMAR
Of the LATIN TONGUE.
By the fame AUTHOR.
Third Edition.   Price One Shilling and Sixpence.

———————

5. BISCHOFF's NOMENCLATOR:
In Latin, French, and Englifh.
Octavo.   Price Two Shillings and Sixpence.

———————

6. SELECT PASSAGES FROM VARIOUS
AUTHORS.—By a LADY.
Defigned to form the Minds and Manners of Young Perfons.
Price Three Shillings and Sixpence bound.

www.ingramcontent.com/pod-product-compliance
Lightning Source LLC
Chambersburg PA
CBHW021117270326
41929CB00009B/920